CW00392592

91 Colette: Le Blé en herbe *and* La Chatte

Critical Guides to French Texts

EDITED BY ROGER LITTLE, WOLFGANG VAN EMDEN, DAVID WILLIAMS

COLETTE

Le Blé en herbe
and
La Chatte

Margaret M. Callander

Senior Lecturer in French
University of Birmingham

Grant & Cutler Ltd
1992

ISBN 0 7293 0340 3

I.S.B.N. 84-599-3274-5
DEPÓSITO LEGAL: V. 749 - 1992

Printed in Spain by
Artes Gráficas Soler, S.A., Valencia
for
GRANT & CUTLER LTD
55-57 GREAT MARLBOROUGH STREET, LONDON W1V 2AY

Contents

For Lesley

Note

Page references in the text are to the following editions: *Le Blé en herbe* (Paris: Garnier-Flammarion, 1969) and *La Chatte* (Paris: Livre de poche, 1989). These are numbered *1* and *2* in the Bibliography, but, for convenience, these two numbers have been dropped where there is no ambiguity in Chapters 3 and 4.

1. Critical Attitudes

From the very first, critics have been mesmerised by the personality of Colette, a construct which, in its public dimension, combined spontaneity and artifice, instinctual wisdom and sophistication, inextricably. This has made it difficult for any sustained and undivided attention to be paid to her literary works, either together or singly. In any case, these works so often draw more or less overtly on biographical experience, and present what may be the same data in such complex and varied forms, that the temptation to try to extract from the sixty-odd volumes a 'real' Colette is very compelling. Indeed, at one level that is exactly what Colette was herself undertaking by writing them at all: the discovery or creation of a coherent self through an evocation of the past, and by reference to other forms of life, human, animal and vegetative. But between this narcissistic quest and autobiography there can be seen to be a divide.

Many literary critics, then, have accepted novels and personal meditations alike as directly confessional in intention and in fact, while biographers have drawn constantly and indiscriminately on her writings as their factual evidence. It is only during the last twenty years that scrutiny of Colette's works as literary objects has been able to develop freely, if unevenly, and, ironically, some of this interest is due to two works which again focused on her life: Michèle Sarde's *Colette, libre et entravée* of 1978, the fullest and most ambitious of the biographies, with a marked social and feminist dimension, and Robert Phelps's ingenious *Earthly Paradise* of 1966, a patchwork of selections from all types of Colette's writing, fiction, anecdote, reminiscence, description and letter, arranged chronologically in what is termed 'an autobiography'. The success of this compilation, likewise of his *Belles Saisons* of 1978, leading towards a theatrical show and attracting many reviews, reawakened interest in Colette as a person, but also, by implication, drew attention to her writing. A considerable investigation and reassessment is now under way, a kind of liberation of Colette's works from critical stereotypes, achieved through a variety of approaches, feminist, thematic, structuralist, sociopolitical.

Colette's work tended, over the years, to generate extreme responses, from outraged hostility to platitudinous adulation, both of these attitudes ultimately patronising and belittling. Julien Benda must have felt that he had eliminated Colette from consideration once and for all by pronouncing that since she had no experience of Latin in her education she could not hope to rank as a French writer. This did not prevent him, however, from multiplying his attacks, desperate as he was to check a shift in values that he discerned towards the cult of sensation, emotion and immediacy. His stance is overtly misogynistic. '*Toute l'esthétique moderne est faite pour les femmes. Les hommes luttent. Beaucoup essayent d'imiter la littérature de leurs rivales. Il faut qu'ils se résignent; il y a un degré d'inintellectualité et d'impudeur qu'ils n'atteindront pas*' (*Belphégor*, 1974, p.114). This kind of charge, directed at Colette with more or less of personal venom, becomes a familiar one. Supporters of Willy, her collaborator and first husband, were quick to suggest that when she wilfully withdrew from his lucid and disciplined influence her writing declined into self-indulgent maunderings. Jean de Pierrefeu, like Benda, saw her as actively hastening the end of civilisation as he knew it. 'Cet art de la sensation dont Colette est le représentant le plus qualifié ... conduit à la nuit cérébrale, à la fin de toute culture, à l'appauvrissement définitif de la personne humaine ramenée au rang de l'animal' (*Journal des Débats*, 13 October, 1920). This particular view is part of the rear-guard action vigorously fought by a number of intellectuals against writers like Gide and Colette who could be seen to be abandoning intellectual and moral structures and any kind of spiritual dimension. Not only are they seen to promote a limited, mechanistic human model, but they simultaneously betray a whole developed, sophisticated literary tradition by their regressive art.

It seems that in Colette's case readers have been disturbed not only by a family of characters whose banal concerns are motivated by patterns of sensation and sentiment alone, but particularly by a narrative voice that does not convey any perceptible satirical, ideological, or moral view of the phenomena presented. This has disconcerted many people, and suspicion has persisted well beyond the establishment of the conventions of the *nouveau roman* and other radical changes in the strategies of fiction-writing. In 1961 Henri Peyre was castigating Colette as both 'antediluvian' and 'always grossly overrated'. He singled her out, with Giraudoux, as 'the most insidious corruptors of taste in our age', and his personal distaste emerges clearly in his repudiation of her masculine characters: 'It is not surprising that many males should refuse to recognize themselves in those men who have little brain and less heart and whose introspective life is so elementary' (*Yale French Studies*, 27, 1961). And these are by no means the last shots in the locker. Attenuated expressions of unease are still audible. Marina Warner in 1983: 'She seems to us now rather bound within her rapidly dating vanity fair on the one hand and her sensuous pastoralism on the other — and her concerns are repetitive' (*Sunday Times*, 19 June, 1983).

It is probable that some of this suspicion was created, or hardened, by the extraordinary cult of 'notre grande Colette' that established itself by the 1920s. Its basic component is her country origin, her love of animals and plants, her passionate attention to natural phenomena, her cultivation of traditional lore. But its strength comes from the tensions between this earth-wisdom and the sophistication of a long-term Paris-dweller, between a personality deemed 'natural' and the elaborate inventions of a very rich and finished style. It is clear that this image satisfied some obscure needs in the French public, and reassured it about certain aspects of the status and function of the writer. Colette was so often photographed in the informal intimacy of her home or gardens, in sandals and surrounded by animals, and interviews confirmed the expectation of a vivid, idiosyncratic, non-intellectual train of speech, that a consonance was established between life-style and artistic production, to many people much more agreeable than that dichotomy between writer and work posited by Proust as being the norm to any outward gaze. She seemed, also, to be laying claim, unaggressively, to a whole area of purely feminine concerns and bringing to bear on them a specifically feminine sensibility. Hence her place in literature would be a special one, and would offer no challenge to masculine achievement. Furthermore, she seemed to have transcended some deep-rooted dialectic of the urban and the pastoral in the French consciousness by linking the energy and adaptability of the one to the conservatism and physicality of the other. She by-passed the pitfalls of the regional novel by the particular nature of her reminiscences, lucid in their pursuit of truth through memory, but full of mysteries and unspoken ambiguities.

All of Colette's surroundings and possessions were invested with a special sanctified aura, and exclamations of wonder would celebrate them. 'Une porte s'ouvre: boudoir! cellule douillette! sanctuaire! c'est le studio de Colette' (Paul Leroy, *Femmes d'aujourd'hui*, 1936, p.18). That Colette herself connived at this myth-making is obvious. Her first question, when she joins this particular interivewer, is 'Que dit La Chatte?' (ibid., p.22). She was by then adept at turning away malicious, importunate or embarrassing questions, and her answer to the query about her lack of Latin culture, the answer that so infuriated Benda, is a masterpiece of provocative evasion, combining the disconcerting and the expected in a simulated spontaneity. 'Je ne sais pas, moi. Je n'ai jamais songé à cela. Il fait chaud ici, je suis bien' (*Mercure de France*, 1 December, 1911).

As for Colette the writer, we can watch critic after critic, perspicacious and experienced though they may be, become enmeshed in the toils of the criteria of 'naturalness' or 'sincerity' that they have set up for themselves as appropriate measures of her art. And, above all, the cult of her style as seamless, miraculous utterance inhibited sustained analysis of her techniques. At the end of a fairly searching study Jean Larnac writes self-deprecatingly:

> Une oeuvre comme la sienne est inclassable. Elle naît
> à l'écart des théories et des cénacles. Elle résiste à

> l'analyse. On ne peut que l'admirer. Goûtons-la donc,
> sans trop chercher à comprendre notre ivresse.
> Je l'ai essayé. J'ai échoué. (*31*, p.225)

Gonzague Truc, for his part, congratulates himself on never having met Colette, and so having some hope of retaining his objectivity (*45*), and René Labou's admonition 'Résistons à la tentation d'écrire que l'oeuvre de Colette représente une espèce de miracle' (*Le Roman français depuis 1900*, 1947, p.19) has a Canute-like ring.

When Colette died in 1954 attention was once more drawn to personal circumstance when the Archbishop of Paris forbade her a Christian burial-service, and Graham Greene wrote his open letter of protest. The publicity that had attended her three marriages and two divorces, her music-hall appearances, her lesbian relationships, was recalled. But her literary reputation did not go into a decline, as so often happens. Rather, it was petrified in the old moulds. Reappraisal came, eventually, through people who had not made the pilgrimage to the celebrated Palais-Royal apartment. It came when Angela Carter was able to assess her as 'a profoundly disingenuous person' (*22*, p.174), and Jacqueline Giry could write 'Colette, pour qui l'écriture est l'acte le plus nécessaire et le plus lucide, a cherché à travers une oeuvre dont la structure est faussement narrative, à établir une multiplicité de dialogues, puis un semblant de discours dont l'enchaînement logique ne la leurre pas' (*29*, p.7).

With authors for whom there is a very rich and varied critical tradition, Marxist, feminist or deconstructionist techniques may seem only complementary. But in Colette's case it is the opening out of a whole range of possibilities previously tapped by only a few pioneers. The recurring charge that Colette presents us with shallow portraits of (in any case) inferior men is deflected by Marcelle Biolley-Godino's dense and detailed study of man as sexual object (*18*). An equally serious and comprehensive investigation is made by Yannick Resch (*40*) into the presentation of the female body and identity. British writers had continued to write sympathetic and unsensational appreciations of Colette's life and work (Margaret Crosland, Margaret Davies, Yvonne Mitchell) and after Elaine

Marks's pioneer work of 1961 (*34*) interest developed in the United
States too. Biography can now range from the painstaking
documentation of Michèle Sarde to the elegant sinuosity of Nicole
Ward Jouve's meditation on the identity of the 'Colette' who is
author, narrator, and character in her own work (*46*). It is Ward
Jouve, incidentally, who offers us the frank testimony of a conver-
sion. From accepting a conventional French view of Colette's writing
as frivolous and unimportant she swung round, as she began reading,
to an absorbed and sustained interest. If Anglo-Saxon attitudes tend
towards the bland, a thread of narrow bias is present in French reactions.

But the general picture is a positive one. The tight elegant
patterns of the novels lend themselves very favourably to structuralist analysis; the complex levels of discourse and the ambivalent
narrative voice of autobiographical material reward investigation;
and the adoption of female specificity, female 'space' as a starting-
point lead to valuable definitions of Colette's attitudes and vocabulary. In the critical dimension, her work has come of age.

2. Starting-points and Focuses

Childhood

Colette is not a writer whose values are fixed in the past. But she does attribute certain qualities to children's experience in general, and her own in particular, that give recollections of early life a unique place in her work. The wider aspect of her perception of children's responses is best seen in her occasional noting of her only daughter's attitudes and development. Of a 'Bel-Gazon' who exclaims as she listens to a hollow nutshell 'Je vois! Je vois la chanson! Elle est aussi fine qu'un cheveu, elle est aussi fine qu'une herbe!', Colette comments

> L'an prochain, Bel-Gazon aura plus de neuf ans. Elle ne
> proclamera plus, inspirée, ces vérités qui confondent ses
> éducateurs. Chaque jour l'éloigne de sa première vie
> pleine, sagace, à toute heure défiante, et qui dédaigne de
> si haut l'expérience, les bons avis, la routinière sagesse.
>
> (*4*, p.1084)

Colette's own childhood self is inseparable from her home at Saint-Sauveur in the Yonne, the garden with its plants, animals and birds, her siblings, her parents, and above all her mother, 'Sido'. The peculiar quality of her 'recherche du temps perdu' did not emerge until *La Maison de Claudine* of 1922, where that mother had been dead for ten years, and it was reinforced by a series of reminiscences, sometimes single sketches, sometimes extended texts, like the *Sido* of 1930, sometimes references in books that appear to have a different focus. These continued until her very last writings, when there was no-one left with whom she could share or check such memories.

What did she select from her childhood for commemoration and appraisal? The sense that she was loved and cherished then in a way that could never be repeated, that she experienced a satisfying harmony of people, animals and plants, that an experimental and humanistic ethic was daily implemented, that she had access to the life of Nature but also to the power of literacy, all of these she relates most closely to the figure of her mother, the member of her family to whom all experiences, all values and even all secrets were ultimately referred.

It is misleading to have the word 'paysanne' so often used of Sidonie Colette, and by extension, her daughter, since this family was by its dress, habits, education and assumptions firmly lodged in the middle class. The animals, birds, insects and plants in which Sido took such a lively and caring interest were those of her own large garden. She cooked and gardened and shopped, but she also kept servants. Colette herself went to the village school, because her mother did not want her to go away from home, but the 'Colette' narrator uses this experience hardly at all, and maintains a distance between the child and the life of the village. There is familiarity, but not intimacy, and the communal experience offers a fascination but also a threat. The excitement of playing for a whole afternoon with other girls, of attending a wedding, disturbs the child, intrudes upon her identity, forces awareness upon her, and she retreats thankfully to the charmed circle of home. In the fictions of the 'Claudine' novels, however, Colette exploited the school experience in a series of racy anecdotes, but even here the Claudine figure remained fiercely private.

Yet the figures of this household were unusual, if not eccentric, and the autobiographical writings distinctly stress the deviance from middle-class conventions that is often a feature of their thinking and their values. Colette celebrates the independence of a mother who takes her dog to mass with her and reads Corneille at boring moments there, who refuses to dismiss a pregnant maid-servant, who leaves the dregs of her bed-time chocolate for a spider to drink. This concern stretches out from the immediate circle, and Colette conveys its urgency:

> ...Il faut soigner cet enfant... Ne peut-on pas sauver cette
> femme? Est-ce que ces gens ont à manger chez eux? Je
> ne peux pourtant pas tuer cette bête... (*4*, p.1002)

Meanwhile, her step-sister retreats into an intensely solipsistic world of dreamy novel-reading, and her brothers, 'les sauvages', demonstrate their practical, logical, non-sociability. It was only much later that Colette pieced together an experimental ethic from these various familiar experiences, based on individual values of independence and endurance. She further endowed her mother with a kind of mythical status. Sido had discouraged, but not forbidden, her daughter from following confirmation classes, but Colette emerged, in the end, as no orthodox Christian believer. What does surface finally is an underlying fascination with the idea of astrology, and a strong sense of the numinous.

The young Colette's belief in her mother's powers is gently satirised in later writings, but there is no doubt that the image of a kind of garden-deity was never toppled in her imagination. Her mother presides over this world of plants, insects, birds and sky, but her continuing preoccupation with the seasons and her sure instinct for weather and winds is the predominant factor in Colette's memory.

> Mon imagination, mon orgueil enfantins situaient notre
> maison au centre d'une rose de jardins, de vents, de
> rayons, dont aucun secteur n'échappait tout à fait à
> l'influence de ma mère. (*8*, p.15)

This awareness of compass-points and winds-directions Colette never lost, through all her urban years; the position of her bed, the dawn detection of the day's wind-speed, these remained matters of urgent importance. Richard (*41*) further cites the miraculous-seeming rain of tiny frogs on to the pregnant Sido as an instance of her multiple involvement with fertility, reflected in the endless recurrence of new animal life among the many domestic animals. Suspicious of marriage as the institutionalised 'theft' of a child, Sido nevertheless fiercely championed the maternal bond. 'Emporte ton faix, ma fille, non pas loin de moi, mais loin de cet homme, et ne le revois plus!' she imagines herself saying to a pregnant daughter, 'Ton malheur commence au moment où tu acceptes d'être la femme d'un malhonnête homme, ta faute est d'espérer qu'il peut te rendre un foyer, l'homme qui t'a détournée du tien' (*4*, p.1048).

What of Colette's father, meanwhile? The captain emerges as a much more enigmatic and marginal figure. On the surface he was a vigorous, open and impetuous southerner, frustrated but not embittered when he lost a leg in the Italian campaigns of Napoleon III, a devoted husband and only secondarily a father. Colette notes his failure to make contact with animals and remembers her stern criticism of his public oratory in local election meetings, but only touches on the chronic financial mismanagement that lost the family the mother's considerable income and assets and led directly to bankruptcy and the break with Saint-Sauveur. Like her mother, she does not overtly question his role as head of the household. But she took to heart Sido's strictures on people who invest all their being in one overriding passion, and her regret for her husband's lost chances of self-fulfilment. 'Ah! quel enfant. Quel dommage qu'il m'ait tant aimée!' (*7*, p.169).

Colette was the passive companion of her father's electoral campaigns, as she was later to accompany her elder brother Achille on his medical rounds and then her first husband in his evening visits to his newspaper offices. She never expected to have a career, and marriage for her was the only exit from a constrained provincial existence. The husband who unexpectedly appeared and took her, dowerless as she was, at the age of twenty, from the new family home with Achille at the village of Châtillon-Coligny, was fourteen years older than herself, and satisfied in some ways what was obviously a need for a tutelary father-figure. But although she seems to have taken her father very much for granted, she much later began to speculate about his inner life and to weigh up what she might have inherited from him. 'Cela me semble étrange, à présent, que je l'aie si peu connu', she wrote in 1929 (*8*, p.35), in the context of a long process of self-appraisal. Her own mature experience allowed her to penetrate retrospectively the jaunty mask of joke and song to sense the melancholy beneath, and to begin to understand the bizarre fantasy that left behind on the captain's shelves a row of neatly-titled and dedicated volumes of memoirs, their pages totally blank. That Colette should first have married a man who, although an industrious and able journalist, never completed a work of creative writing without the help of the band of bondsmen to whom he farmed out sections of his multiple projects, must seem a remarkable coincidence. Since her own early literary activities were at the instigation of Willy and so much under his control that his was the sole name on the covers of the first half-dozen publications, her sense of writing as a forceful and self-determining process developed slowly and hesitantly.

Paris and marriage

Colette's marriage to Henry Gauthier-Villars lasted from 1893 until their legal separation in 1905. Nothing could have been more different from her quiet unsophisticated provincial existence than the life that she led in the artistic and often raffish circles where 'Willy' was a popular figure. This plump and affable man talked endlessly, joked, laughed, fantasised, socialised; but he worked hard under pressure, if only to shore up his elusive finances. Through him Colette met writers, painters, musicians, actors, and eventually learned to write on her own account. Finally she gained the confidence to leave him and to seek a way of being independent. She wrote her own books, she trained as a mime artist and toured the music-halls, she entered upon a lesbian relationship with 'Missy', the Marquise de Belboeuf.

It was not until 1936, in *Mes apprentissages*, that Colette wrote openly about this marriage, and in spite of the lapse of time a residual bitterness is perceptible beneath the reflective and ironic tone. It was not so much Willy's frequent infidelities that wore her down, but the web of deceit and fiction that he so compulsively threw out, together with the penchant for self-publicity and for sexual titillation that made his sexuality seem both shallow and depraved to her. Yet the marital experience was more mixed, more companionate than it is often made out to be, just as the literary collaboration of the spouses was a more complex matter than their respective champions wished to acknowledge. Colette contrived to suggest revulsion from the arch and knowing tone of the 'Claudine' novels, while at the same time claiming the books as essentially her own. Certainly she had become wearied at the relentless publicity propagated around them by her husband.

But Colette judged her own earlier attitudes harshly: 'Une coupable griserie, un affreux et impur élan d'adolescente' (*9*, p.42) is what she detected in her life as in her novels. It was important to her to feel cleansed, and she achieved this by, for instance, writing about animals, just before the separation, in the first book that she signed with her own name (Colette Willy), and for which she received the accolade of a preface by Francis Jammes. 'Je me donnai le plaisir, non point vif, mais honorable, de ne pas parler de l'amour' (*9*, p.141) she wrote of *Dialogues de bêtes*.

Her perception of lesbianism was also, at this time, part of the impulse towards purity and wholeness, a theme developed later in the subtle and complex *Le Pur et l'impur* of 1932. This emerged in the delicate, intense lyricism of *Les Vrilles de la vigne*, where Colette was developing the allusive power of imagery, and her preoccupation is reflected in Renée's comment on her lover Max's insensitivity in *La Vagabonde* of 1910.

> Deux femmes enlacées ne seront jamais pour lui qu'un groupe polisson, et non l'image mélancolique et touchante de deux faiblesses, peut-être réfugiées aux bras l'une de l'autre pour y dormir, y pleurer, fuir l'homme souvent méchant, et goûter, mieux que tout plaisir, l'amer bonheur de se sentir pareilles, infimes, oubliées... (*3*, p.1207)

Another source of strength was the company of theatre folk. Colette never faltered in her respect and admiration towards her companions of this period. She valued their stubborn endurance, honour, loyalty and modesty. She is touched by 'cette obligeance discrète et désin-téressée, cette réserve timide et courtoise qui semble avoir sa patrie dans les seules coulisses du music-hall' (*4*, p.309) that soothed and supported her, and contributed towards this time of renewal and reorientation.

By 1910, however, these kinds of activities and preoccupations began to be overlapped by a new set which heralded Colette's emergence as a fully professional writer and journalist. She began to publish regularly in *Le Matin*, the newspaper of which Henry de Jouvenel, her second husband, was one of the editors, just before the purchase of 'Rozven', the house in Brittany which was to have offered a lasting refuge to herself and Missy. There followed a sequence of powerfully-felt events that called upon her newly-devel-oped resources, the death of her mother, her marriage into an old-established aristocratic family, the birth of her only child, Colette de Jouvenel, the First World War. Colette emerged a mature woman, a writer to be reckoned with, an able hostess, who kept hospitable and open house, particularly at Rozven, for daughter, stepchildren, friends and associates. Hers was the style which regulated the way of life in Paris and in Brittany, but she baulked at the role of political hostess, and, as her husband moved further into his important politi-cal identity, this, and the emotional storms of their marriage, drove them apart and led to their separation in 1924.

During the period of this marriage Colette retained her signa-ture of Colette Willy, reached the important post of literary editor of *Le Matin*, and continued her association with the theatre. Now she acted in plays, particularly as Léa in an adaptation of *Chéri*, and she also began to go on lecture tours. She was in no way a conventional society wife, and the transition to living alone did not leave her bereft of occupation or status.

This was the period of her most assured and ambitious fictional enterprises. The probing intense search for identity of the first-person novels *La Vagabonde* and *L'Entrave* gave way in the

twenties to the sequence of third-person narratives for which Colette
is best known, *Chéri, La Fin de Chéri, Le Blé en herbe, La Seconde,
La Chatte, Duo, Le Toutounier, Julie de Carneilhan*. These represent
a formidable achievement in terms of varied narrative technique and
mature interpretation of emotional states. Adolescent girls, married
women, independent and ageing women, all are seen to reveal a
toughness, a will to survival that carries them through humiliating
and exhausting circumstances. Their strategies are not identical:
Julie and Alice return to their childhood homes, Edmée and Camille
claim independence, Vinca assumes responsibility for the couple,
Léa takes on the assertive and sexless identity which is her only
means of cancelling out the image of the successful courtesan. The
men are emotionally more frail — Michel and Chéri sink into a
lethargic despair that ends in suicide, Alain's return home is dangerously regressive, Farou, Phil, Herbert do not, in the end, triumph
over the women whom they appear to dominate. Yet the balance is
not one-sided and no character achieves happiness; lucid awareness
and the will to go forward, an appreciation of the choices that are
possible, a sense of relativity, these capacities may develop in an
otherwise shallow and lethargic consciousness, but this is enough to
set up moving or ironic resonances of loss and exile, yearning and
isolation.

In the thirties Colette led a life that was at once more with-
drawn, as her companionship with Maurice Goudeket developed
quietly, and more public, as she travelled enthusiastically, wrote
material based on these travels and on, for instance, a series of
murder trials, opened a beauty salon, became a dramatic critic. The
axis of her living changed after she deserted Brittany for a house in
Provence, 'La Treille Muscate', near Saint-Tropez. She was finally
able to move into the flat in the rue de Beaujolais that is so
intimately associated with her, and the Palais-Royal became her final
home. Sequestered there by rheumatism, by the war, by Goudeket's
imprisonment, she became a renowned, an almost mythical figure.

In 1922 Colette had begun to consolidate the short pieces that
form the re-creation of her childhood that she chose to call *La
Maison de Claudine*, followed by *Sido* and complemented by other

isolated sketches in the same mode, fictionalised reminiscence. This was at once the re-creation of a lost era and the pursuit of evidence about her own identity, consolidated not only by a self-portrait but by an investigation of her father, mother, siblings, animals, neighbours. Another type of self-awareness is pursued through the light fictional web of *La Naissance du jour* (1928), where a 'Colette' figure achieves a *Rosenkavalier*-like renunciation of sexual passion and a reassessment of self that is closely linked to a portrait of Sido. The narrator envisages a richer life, an equality of the sexes, a harmony with Nature, all evolving from her acceptance of the ageing process. The various novellas and the reflective volumes that became the favoured literary modes of Colette's later years also use a 'Colette' narrator to ruminate on the strange behaviour of her fellow humans, drawing no conclusions, but constantly placing experience, dialogues, characters under the magnifying glass of a keen perception. Stewart emphasises how much 'the fabulations are subtle and difficult to delimit' (*44*, p.111), how much they are 'less revelations of the author than part of a codified aesthetic structure'. So the shift was finally away from conventional narrative fiction and towards these flexible and experimental forms of reflective writing, where the seemingly banal and insignificant is woven into a pattern of allusion and resonance.

Passion and nature

As a revelation of Colette's view of sexual passion Jacqueline Giry (*29*) selects 'La Main' from the only collection of 'conventional' short stories, *La Femme cachée* of 1924. A young wife contemplates her sleeping husband's hand on the sheets, and it is at first detached, then isolated, a horrifying, coarse, spider-like organism. All the ambiguity of her sexual response focuses on this object, as she deliberately opts for acceptance.

> Puis elle cacha sa peur, se dompta courageusement, et commençant sa vie de duplicité, de résignation, de

> diplomatie vile et délicate, elle se pencha, et baisa
> humblement la main monstrueuse. (*6*, p.43)

Sexuality may be natural, but it is consistently presented by Colette as a dangerous temptation, a bondage, a shackle (as in *L'Entrave* of 1913), a debilitating fever, a loss of integrity. Realisation of its power is, as in 'La Main', degrading and alarming, and it dooms the woman, in particular, to a course of deceit and painful self-abnegation; the inevitability of this alienation is unfolded as fatalistically as in any medieval romance. 'L'amour, ce n'est pas un sentiment honorable' Colette quotes her mother as saying (*7*, p.56), and it is the terrifying, exhausting cost of passion that she so often displays in her writing: death for some, diminution for others, pain for all.

One of the strengths of childhood for Colette is its sturdy wholeness. 'Vous n'imaginez pas quelle reine de la terre j'étais à douze ans!' she says in *Les Vrilles de la vigne*, and in analysing this state she emphasises its androgyny.

> Mais ce que j'ai perdu, Claudine, c'est mon bel orgueil,
> la secrète certitude d'être une enfant précieuse, de sentir
> en moi une âme extraordinaire d'homme intelligent, de
> femme amoureuse, une âme à faire éclater mon petit
> corps. (*3*, pp.1032-33)

Colette sees puberty as a kind of fall into the constraints of sexuality, and this forms a very apt illustration of Simone de Beauvoir's dictum 'On ne naît pas femme: on le devient' (*Le Deuxième Sexe*, Gallimard, 1949, I, p.285). It is particularly the girl child that Colette is thinking of; it is she who has most to lose. But puberty is by no means unproblematical for the male, and its strains have physical effects: Phil and Jean (*La Seconde*) faint, Toni (*Julie de Carneilhan*) attempts suicide. In early manhood this sensitivity will be blunted; but its underlying effects can resurface, as we see when Chéri and Michel die. Chéri and Alain seem dangerously arrested in their adolescent mould. But Colette allows women characters to double back towards childhood with much less of diminishment. This movement represents a search for security, but also for strength and resilience. The widowed Alice goes back to the flat in Paris that is dominated by the 'toutounier', the enormous divan that is the sisters' symbolic domain. Julie de Carneilhan breaks away from her emotional bondage to Herbert, and the complicity with him that ends in humiliation and deceit, to return with her brother to their country home, a rougher but cleaner existence. Renée is strengthened in her decision to remain a 'vagabonde' by travelling through the country-side of her youth and conjuring up images of her child self, 'la longue enfant qui traînait ici ses royales tresses, et sa silencieuse humeur de nymphe des bois' (*3*, p.1198) — again, the regal metaphor and the sense of a secret, inner robustness.

This identity is often seen to co-exist with what then can seem the alien presence of an overwhelming sensuality, and this is conveyed through a technique of *dédoublement*. As an excited and half-drunk Claudine babbles out her love to Renaud, 'la Claudine sage s'efface timidement, admirative et respectueuse, devant l'autre, qui est allée droit où le Destin la poussait, sans se retourner, comme une conquérante ou une condamnée' (*3*, p.362). Renée feels more resentment and alarm at the passive tenacity of

> ce corps de femme allongé qui me barre la route, un voluptueux corps aux yeux fermés, volontairement aveugle, étiré, prêt à périr plutôt que de quitter le lieu de sa joie... C'est moi, cette femme-là, cette brute entêtée au plaisir. (*3*, p.1217)

The idea of being driven by some kind of uncontrollable force that might well be termed 'destiny' is powerfully illustrated in the animal stories, which can be seen as oblique explorations of phenomena like sexual passion, using a genre in which the narrator can be more direct or more lyrical than when dealing with humans, or so Colette seems to have felt. When Forestier (*28*) is attempting to analyse the apparently random placing of the sketches in *La Maison de Claudine* and to account for the enigmatic nature of some of them, he notes the central positioning of 'La Toutouque', and its significance in relation

to themes of passion, jealousy and mystery. This cheerful, affection-
ate, unbeautiful dog is seen as a trusting appendage to the family,
until the moment when her lust and jealousy turn her into an
unrecognisable yellow projectile, 'une bête jaune, masquée de noir,
garnie de dents, d'yeux exorbités , d'une langue violacée où écumait
la salive' (*4*, p.1032). It is through the eyes of a ten year-old Colette
that this monstrous transformation is perceived, as well as
Toutouque's shamed attempt to conceal this imperative from the
humans, and hers is the startled inconclusive response to this
phenomenon.

> — Oh! Toutouque... Toutouque...
> Je ne trouvais pas d'autres paroles, et ne savais comment
> me plaindre, m'effrayer et m'étonner qu'une force
> malfaisante, dont le nom même échappait à mes dix ans,
> pût changer en brute féroce la plus douce des créatures.

This episode is integrated into the pattern of *La Maison de Claudine*,
where a brief intense focus shifts from scene to scene and forward
and back in time, moving around the family and its locale, and
extending to other participants, other scenes, before returning again
to its centre. Links are not made overtly, conclusions are not drawn,
but each episode reinforces the others by some means. The earlier
decision to bring together a number of pieces as *Les Vrilles de la
vigne* has a similar effect. A series of explorations of possible
stances, possible identities, has a group of animal sketches as its
centre, and the story of 'Nonoche' is another exemplary fable. It
catches the moment when the proud devoted mother of a fat complacent male kitten thrusts aside this astonished princeling to walk away
into the woods at evening in response to the irresistible summons of
the tom-cat. Here the wail of the tom is transmuted by the narrator
into a rhetorical discourse where Colette can insert her own perception of the stark power of sexuality.

> Mes flancs vides se touchent et ma peau glisse autour de
> mes muscles secs, entraînés au rapt et au viol... Et toute

cette laideur me fait pareil à l'Amour! Viens!... Quand je
paraîtrai à tes yeux, tu ne reconnaîtras rien de moi... que
l'Amour!

Mes dents courberont ta nuque rétive, je souillerai ta
robe, je t'infligerai autant de morsures que de caresses,
j'abolirai en toi le souvenir de ta demeure et tu seras,
pendant des jours et des nuits, ma sauvage compagne
hurlante... jusqu'à l'heure plus noire où tu te retrouveras
seule, car j'aurai fui mystérieusement, las de toi, appelé
par celle que je ne connais pas, celle que je n'ai pas
possédée encore. (*3*, pp.991-92)

In an *œuvre* where a considerable reserve is maintained in the
depiction of sexual scenes and where fictional characters are seldom
eloquent, these are means by which inner perceptions can be exteriorised through stylised allusion, but still harmonised with a plausible
animal psychology. It is not that Colette cannot depict relationships
between men and women as enriching, enlivening, light-hearted,
warm, instructive and stimulating, and certainly they are complex.
She herself seems curious, fascinated, wary, disturbed, repelled, but
the source of her *malaise* is often located actively in the male. In a
letter of 1921 she reflects

J'ai acquis depuis bien longtemps la conviction que toute
présence masculine active — c'est à dire l'homme aimé,
l'homme qui peut être aimé, l'homme qui veut l'être —
est, à de certains et de nombreux moments, nocive.

As someone who was very receptive to the presence and identity of
others she seems convinced of the transmission of a material influence, 'une espèce de poison, excitant ou accablant' (*25*, pp.152-53).
Small wonder, then, that the resolutions of *La Naissance du jour*, the
choice by a middle-aged 'Colette' of solitariness, taps a flow of relief,
joy and serenity in a woman who had almost forgotten that a man

could be an unthreatening equal and a sharer. 'Adieu, cher homme, et bienvenue aussi à toi' (*7*, p.57).

The 'natural' is difficult to define in Colette's work. It has been partly obscured by the stereotypes of Colette that admirers have endorsed: the earth-mother, the sensualist, the peasant, the child of Nature. A favoured view is that Colette, who was a skilled cook and gardener, really preferred such activities, so that writing was a sideline or a financial necessity. Another variant decrees that her writing is essentially 'natural'. These images are derived partly as deduction from her fiction and partly because she did not contradict such views of herself consistently, but tolerated them as a form of camouflage. It would certainly be wrong to see her as unthinkingly accepting all aspects of the life of Nature, still less as responding in any unsophisticated way to its savageries. Claudine turns away when Fanchette's kittens are born; the adolescent Colette faints when she reads Zola's account of child-birth in *La Terre*. There is so much intensity of response to natural scenes, so much curiosity and pleasure, such power of evoking beauty, radiance, singularity, complexity, minuteness, that it does often seem as though Colette is recording a universe that is not only fascinating but benign. This would be misleading, however. The beloved shrubs of the Saint-Sauveur garden choke each other, collapse under their own weight, and the wistaria has torn the iron railings from their seating. Bloomberg (*19*) has traced images of wistaria through Colette's work, and notes their consistently sinister and aggressive connotations. Episodes that are lively and charming sometimes carry curious contradictions. As she watches a blackbird pillaging her precious cherries Sido is seized by 'une sorte de frénésie riante' (*8*, p.171), a thrill of admiration for the bold, free violence of this handsome predator. Another surprising response, this time to a human situation, is recorded from the point of view of a fifteen-year-old 'Colette' in 'Le Sieur Binard'. This apparent reminiscence portrays a country family where the widowed patriarch impregnates his daughters as they reach puberty, and Sido's attitude to this situation is a mixed one. She muses to her daughter:

> Leur maison est très bien tenue... L'enfant de la petite a
> des cils longs comme ça... je l'ai vue l'autre jour, elle
> allaitait son bébé sur le pas de la porte, c'était ravissant...
> Qu'est-ce que je dis? C'était abominable quand on est au
> courant, naturellement... (*5*, XI, p.278)

The placing and the significance of 'naturellement' is enigmatic. The
social response is a shocked one, but Sido's first reaction is to a vital,
traditional appropriateness. And, of course, there are no husbands
here.

Colette's elective landscape was the lonely, shadowy woods
around Saint-Sauveur, not pretty, not grand, and certainly not open.
She sought to lose herself in 'le vert velouté des bois' (*3*, p.8),
responding to textures, smells, tastes. In Paris Claudine is homesick
for 'l'odeur musquée et pourrie de feuilles mortes' (*3*, p.231); the
woods represent security, coolness, fertility.

> J'errai donc dans les chemins pattés [boueux] dans les
> bois rouillés, parfumés de champignons et de mousses
> mouillées, récoltant des girolles jaunes, amies des sauces
> crémeuses et du veau à la casserole. (*3*, p.225)

Colette responded later to the living power of the sea, and she came
to love the aromatic warmth of Provence. But she often recalled with
precision and intensity her childhood forest world and the ritualistic
nature of her walks, the compulsion that took her, for instance, at
dawn to certain cherished springs.

> La première avait goût de feuille de chêne, la seconde de
> fer et de tige de jacinthe... Rien qu'à parler d'elles je
> souhaite que leur saveur m'emplisse la bouche au
> moment de tout finir, et que j'emporte avec moi, cette
> gorgée imaginaire. (*8*, p.164)

In these damp, enclosed, but untrammelled spaces Colette felt her
most intuitive tie with the earth; but, in Proustian manner, she found

expression for this in adulthood, and when the experience was part of her past. Colette did not erect a theory of memory in her work, but she never lost the ability to respond to her mother's urgently repeated imperative, 'Regarde!'

Writing

Colette often reverted to the theme of her lack of artistic vocation, and stressed the idea that she had come to writing by chance. She worked it into her formal *discours de réception* at the Belgian Royal Academy, where it made a piquant contrast to memories of her predecessor, that total lyricist Anna de Noailles. 'Je suis devenue écrivain sans m'en apercevoir, et sans que personne s'en doutât' (*5*, XIII, p.446). In fact, Colette congratulates herself elsewhere that no such ambition or imperative troubled her adolescence. She is convinced that the self-consciousness involved in self-expression would have interfered with the integrity of her perceptions.

> Quelle douceur j'ai pu goûter à une telle absence de vocation littéraire! Mon enfance, ma libre et solitaire adolescence, toutes deux préservées du souci de m'exprimer, furent toutes deux occupées uniquement de diriger leurs subtiles antennes vers ce qui se contemple, s'écoute, se palpe et se respire. (*10*, p.126)

But one thing that this childhood did contain was books. Classic authors were read continually, avidly, and it would be quite wrong to consider Colette uneducated or unlettered. Balzac, for instance, became a lifelong bedside presence. At fifteen, Colette is amazed to hear a neighbour declare that Balzac is hard going. 'Balzac ardu? lui, mon berceau, ma forêt, mon voyage?' (*5*, XII, p.249). The metaphoric connection with other nurturing and sustaining elements is striking. For her brothers and herself, particularly, there was a special and considered place for 'la lecture forcenée et ses muets délires' (*10*, p.144), so satisfying to the adolescent imagination; but a line is drawn between this and the drugged fantasies of Juliette.

Another pleasure of the youthful Colette was in the aural. In 'Le Curé sur le mur' she recounts the transformations of the splendid and obscure word 'presbytère'. 'J'avais recueilli en moi le mot mystérieux, comme brodé d'un relief rêche en son commencement, achevé en une longue et rêveuse syllabe' (*4*, p.986). She tries it out as a solemn curse, applies it to a pretty snail-shell. The discovery of its mundane application daunts her only momentarily, before she has found a way to compromise while retaining her autonomy: the wall shall be the 'presbytère' and she will be its *curé*. The 'sign' is wayward, but in the end it does not disappoint.

Far from writing being an easy or 'natural' occupation for Colette, endless letters and the testimonies of her friends are witness to the gruelling and disciplined nature of her professionalism. Endings in particular gave her difficulty, and the apparently casual and understated phraseology of many of her conclusions is deceptive. Maurice Goudeket comments, 'Capable alors de travailler huit ou dix heures d'affilée, elle ressemblait enfin à un cocon' (*30*, p.22). The holiday periods away from Paris contained their regular writing sessions, for Colette came to regard her art as a kind of obligation. 'Si je n'ai pas la passion, j'ai l'honneur de mon métier', she said to Frédéric Lefèvre in 1927 (*32*, p.133). This, then, is a serious practitioner of the skills of writing, and the feints and sallies of her reactions to criticism should not deceive us.

Another area in which Colette had to defend herself concerned the nature of her writing. To say that her works were one and all autobiographical was a way of denigrating her originality. 'Homme, mon ami, tu plaisantes volontiers les oeuvres, fatalement autobiographiques, de la femme', says the narrator of *La Naissance du jour* (*7*, pp.99-100), and this consideration is one that troubled Colette throughout her career. Critics multiplied their efforts to find *clés* for the characters of the fiction, and although at times there is a strong referential link discernible, at others any transposition is convoluted at the very least. Colette herself is prepared to posit a proleptic element in her creativity, but critics prefer retrospective models. Speculation about the place of Bertrand de Jouvenel in Colette's life and work provides salutary examples of silliness and spite. Because

the physical relationship with Bertrand was categorically denied
until the 1980s, with his brother Renaud, for instance, offering
Yvonne Mitchell in 1975 convincing psychological reasons why no
such affair could possibly have taken place (*36*), rumour attributed to
Colette's stepson a disproportionate inspirational role in her work.
His own testimony is used by the editors of the second volume of the
Pléiade *Œuvres complètes* to scotch the hypothesis that he could in
any way be linked to the character of Chéri. There is, however, a
legitimate parallel to be made in the case of Philippe in *Le Blé en
herbe*, and it is clearly documented that his account of his youthful
friendship with Paméla Paramythioti was significant to Colette. But
Phil's is a much more reserved and conventional figure than Chéri's,
and a less fruitful source of speculation. However, we may note that
the obituary-writer of *The Times* (6 March) was so mesmerised by
this connection that, at Bertrand de Jouvenel's death in 1987, in
addition to the usual identification with Chéri, the authorship of *Le
Blé en herbe* is confidently and extraordinarily attributed to Bertrand
himself. While Bertrand de Jouvenel always spoke of his stepmother
with dignity and probity, those biographers who claim to support
him (Joanna Richardson, Jeannie Malige) use him as the ostensible
basis of their exercises in myth-reversal. As well as appearing hostile
to Colette's personality, they also attack her characterisation through
a 'Morton's fork' approach: Colette was uncreative, and habitually
and wantonly used models from her immediate circle for her
portraitures; however as she was not really as good a writer as she is
cracked up to be, her delineations are unpleasantly distorted. This is
a not unusual argument, but its inconsistencies appear to have
escaped its authors.

Colette does not attempt any systematic defence of her writing
strategies, although her scattered pronouncements are numerous. But
they are often oblique, defensive, exaggerated or provocative. However she did not lack self-confidence. 'Elle avait toutes les vertus de
l'artisan français', Goudeket comments, 'l'humilité, la patience,
l'exigence envers soi, le goût de l'ouvrage achevé' (*30*, p.21). These
solid abilities underpinned the evolution of her style. When Renée is

evoking the feel of creative writing, she describes words and phrases as though they were elusive animals to be tracked and tamed:

> Pourtant, j'avais savouré... la volupté d'écrire, la lutte patiente contre la phrase qui s'assouplit, s'assoit en rond comme une bête apprivoisée, l'attente immobile, l'affût qui finit par *charmer* le mot. (*3*, p.1084)

If we can accept that *la vagabonde* is here speaking with Colette's voice, then we can see the same passionate and technical precision going into the search for words as in her botanical researches or her study of butterflies:

> Je prends encore la plume, pour commencer le jeu périlleux et décevant, pour saisir et fixer, sous la pointe double et ployante, le chatoyant, le fugace, le passion-nant adjectif. (*3*, p.1074)

Renée is describing a vital and mysterious act; it is not the mimicry of a carefully-observed reality, although that element is present in Colette's writing too, but the powerful vivifying of the word, some kind of organic process. It is perhaps in this light that Montherlant's phrase 'Colette, le plus grand écrivain français naturel' should be understood, although it may still appear incongruous, placed as it is on the cover of the Garnier-Flammarion edition of *La Naissance du jour*, Colette's most elaborate and serpentine exercise in ambiguity.

A further challenge or screen is offered by Colette's choice of an authorial signature. Her surname, her father's name, a first-name when she used it in conjunction with 'Willy', and finally the integral title, subsuming all aspects of her life and elements of her personality. Extended through her niece and her daughter, it makes a bid to fill all of her personal space, and on her books it subverts gender distinctions and the need for pseudonyms.

Ward Jouve thinks that some of the puzzles about Colette as author are due to her 'decided indifference to the sacralization of writing' (*46*, p.174), her reverence for it being of a different species.

Certainly writing is used by Colette in idiosyncratic, experimental, subversive and ambivalent ways. Each work is relatively modest in scope and aim, but the whole *œuvre* takes on a startlingly ambitious and challenging air when it is viewed as a pattern.

3. *Le Blé en herbe*

Colette's familiarity with Brittany relates essentially to her regular visits to Rozven, the substantial old house by the sea between Cancale and Paramé which she helped Missy to buy in 1911 and which she left in 1926 when she gave over her allegiance to Provence. Previously the two friends had stayed at Le Crotoy, in Normandy, and Colette's first trip to the sea had been a stay at Belle-Isle in 1894 with her husband Willy. Colette knew Rozven at all its seasons, but her main visits were in the summer months, and her letters testify to her pleasure, excitement and interest. What she sought was relaxation, of course, but this was of a very active nature. For Francis Carco she described how she spent the best part of her time. 'Le reste est pour la mer, le défrichage, la pêche, le lézardisme, et surtout le bain. Carco, cet endroit est incomparable' (*13*, p.215). She appreciated the very secluded position of the house, but it was not precisely solitude that she sought, rather the company of close friends and kindred spirits. Germaine Beaumont, her secretary at *Le Matin*, describes her child-like enthusiasm for their purchases of local antiques and brightly-coloured materials, their bathing-parties and their sea-food meals. She was no passive proprietor, but gardened and planted trees. Although not an expert swimmer she enjoyed the physical struggle with the strong waves. She fished and collected shellfish, and the ignorant curiosity of Belle-Isle days gave place to a detailed appreciation of the botanical resources of the coast. Missy had used Rozven to lap Colette around with comfort and rest between her acting engagements. In her turn Colette saw it as a mission to receive and nurture friends and family, particularly her daughter and her two stepsons. 'Je le frictionne, le gave, le frotte au sable, le brunis au soleil' (*12*, p.53), she says of Bertrand de Jouvenel in 1921. Often, too, she devoted hours to her writing, with that total absorption so often noted by witnesses. Brittany, then, is associated for Colette with an active interplay with the elements of sun, shore and sea, with a kind of robust renewal of body and spirit. Yet one of the most striking images that we have of Colette at Rozven is of still contemplation and solitary enjoyment, a raptness that is another dimension of her response.

> If you would know her, think of a garden in Brittany by the sea. It is early morning and she has been awakened by the melancholy two-note whistling of these birds we call *courlis*: she has come down, carefully by-passing a stack of sleeping cats, and a bulldog has followed her silently. She sits in delightful loneliness on the damp and salty grass and her hand enjoys the roughness of the herbs. The sound of the waves fills her mind, she looks now at them, now at the flowers, which are moving faintly upward as the weight of the dew dissolves.
> (B. de Jouvenel, *Time and Tide*, 14 August, 1954)

Le Blé en herbe is the only novel for which Colette used a Breton setting, and it exploits that period of late summer when holiday-makers begin to consider the return to their urban lives. Margaret Davies sums it up: 'It is the transient essence of holiday at its most poignant and exquisite' (*24*, p.67). But its genesis and formulation were not consistently identified with such a setting. 'Avril', a fragment that Colette did not in the end use for her novel, an episode that would seem to precede in chronology the main action, is set in Paris. But Colette's indication of how she first envisaged 'Le Seuil' (the early title for *Le Blé en herbe*) diverges radically from the novel-form with its developed characters, while emphasising one of the preoccupations of the final work. Using her theatrical experience as actress and mime, she imagines a duologue:

> Le rideau se lève, la scène est plongée dans l'obscurité,
> deux personnages invisibles dissertent sur l'amour avec
> beaucoup de science et d'expérience. Vers les dernières

répliques, on donne la lampe et les spectateurs surpris
s'aperçoivent que les partenaires ont réciproquement
quinze et seize ans. Je voulais signifier par là que
l'amour passion n'a pas d'âge et que l'amour n'a pas deux
espèces de langage. Je n'ai pas dit autre chose dans *Le
Blé en herbe*. J'ai seulement intercalé dans le récit
quelques paysages cancalais qui m'avaient vivement
émue. (*32*, p.139)

So the emphasis has to do with the ageless and universal nature of
sexual passion and its expression. But it is unlikely that readers will
feel the Breton landscapes to have been inserted into the plot. In fact
they are essential to its articulation. The experiences of the adolescent couple are often interpreted for the reader by the narrator's
voice, but they are consistently extended and qualified through the
resonances offered by images of rock, sand, sea and sky, of sun, rain,
night and day.

Another important shift of development occurred because the
novel, published in June 1923, originally appeared as a series of
separate sketches at intervals in *Le Matin* under the heading used by
Colette for her short stories and pieces, 'Contes des mille et un
matins'. There was no overall title, but each 'episode', between 29
July, 1922 and 31 March, 1923, was given its own heading, and
some features of the narrative mode, where there is often a *reprise* of
names and physical characteristics at the start of new sections, most
certainly relate to this serial publication method. But a decision of *Le
Matin*'s editors resulted in the final episodes never appearing in that
newspaper. This was not rupture in mid-sentence, as was later to
happen with *Ces plaisirs* in *Gringoire*, but it did mean that the
emotional climax of the book, the physical union of Vinca and Phil,
was suppressed. Readers were allowed to follow through discreetly
the affair between Madame Dalleray, the conventional 'femme de
trente ans' and the youthful Phil, but an adolescent Vinca entering
into a physical relationship of her own free will was not to be tolerated. This was an unexpected snub to a regular literary contributor,
and an affront to the wife of one of *Le Matin*'s editors. But the ban

persisted. One of its artistic effects was that Colette made almost no further attempt to divide up the last part of the text when she was preparing her novel, and so this longer unified section gains in depth and consistency as the tone of the narrative darkens. This is reinforced by Colette's abandoning of section titles in the final version.

In a novel that has been widely praised, and assessed in very similar terms by many critics, only this ending has proved at all controversial. In early reviews it was sometimes regretted, as a blot upon an otherwise fresh and engaging novel, but subsequently the open-ended nature of the final paragraph has set up ambiguities that have led to divergent interpretations of this development in Phil and Vinca's relationship and by implication differing evaluations of the whole meaning of the text.

Time and place

The topography of this coastal locale is very lightly sketched in, but with a few specific details that identify it closely with Rozven. St Malo is eleven kilometres away, we learn, when Phil cycles there, the headlands of le Nez (p.60) and Granville (p.174) are mentioned, but there are no formalised descriptions of house or shore. The protagonists are moving in a wholly familiar world of repeated and anticipated experiences — the daily bathe, the shrimping expeditions, walks, picnics. Within these limits they are autonomous, and their responsibilities to others are few. Interaction with adults is deliberately played down by ironic reference to the parents as 'Ombres'. To be sure, Vinca sews, looks after her sister Lisette, puts on her best dress and hands round the coffee cups when there are guests to a meal. Sometimes Phil is tolerant of such activities, sometimes obscurely irritated. They accept the family decisions as to their futures, and if they distance themselves it is with a feeling of the unreality of their parents' stance and identity. It would seem absurd to imagine that their parents could have experienced intense and complex emotions (p.78) but they do not go on to claim any rights or privileges, however unique they may feel themselves to be.

The parents are modestly well off, and there are no expensive pleasures, clothes or meals for these children. The props to their drama are well-worn and few, therefore, but their days are full and rich and totally absorbing. When *la dame en blanc* intrudes on this scene her worldly assessment is particularly discordant — 'Une Bretagne modérée, pas très caractéristique, mais reposante' (p.84) — because it is an outside view of a *locus* hitherto completely bound up with the familiar unquestioning perceptions of the main characters. Philippe in fact identifies it intimately in a Proustian recall with Vinca: 'le nom appelait, inséparable de son amie, le souvenir du sable, chaud aux genoux, serré et fuyant au creux des paumes' (p.75). This fusion of time, place and experience is one of the binding agents of the narrative. Time is articulated in a particularly subtle and intricate way. The text covers only the final month of the holiday. A mood of timeless, secure ease has already been established by its start, but the shadow of autumn infuses it with a poignant melancholy. The families will leave on September 25, and the Paris life is predictable. Yet it seems unreal in relation to the familiar pursuits of summer and sea. 'The little love-story is built up on paradox within paradox', Davies comments (*24*, p.64), and this is nowhere more evident than in the persons of the adolescents and their feelings about the present and future. Phil, in particular, is torn between his urgent and exasperated need to break into adulthood: 'Je crève, entends-tu, je crève à l'idée que je n'ai que seize ans!' (p.47), and his need to halt the process of time, to cancel out the unexpected and the unwelcome — 'je lui dirais "Ce n'est pas vrai. Il ne s'est rien passé! Tu es ma Vinca de toujours"' (p.185). He feels that Time diminishes him; he is 'à peu près homme, à peu près libre, à peu près amoureux' (p.47), yet his capitulation to Mme Dalleray dooms him to a master/slave relationship without issue. For Vinca, too, it seems urgently necessary to halt time, if Phil is not to be lost. Yet she is prepared to take a desperate and lonely step into the future, when she draws Phil towards physical union. And these are no static personalities. At all times the narrator stresses the ambivalence of their personalities and their self-perception, their status is defined through their moods and their activities, and they veer from adult conviction and complexity to child-like exuberance, inconsequentiality and vulnerability from scene to scene and from moment to moment. A further ambivalence decrees that the gender-perceptions of the characters should be stereotyped — 'nous, les femmes, enfin' (p.43), and 'tous les garçons de mon âge' (p.168); yet one of the most pervasive techniques of the writing is explicitly to break down and subvert gender definitions in describing the young people. Their age and their particular physique makes this possible as a recurring descriptive mode. Vinca's coltishness and Phil's neat smoothness are exaggerated in times of stress into severity and frailty. Sometimes one personality will dominate, at others its partner. Characteristics can be exchanged, submerged, sharpened. This fluidity, matched by the flux of the sea and the lightening and darkening of the sky, creates a subtle shifting ground-work to the simple dialogues and actions.

Vinca

Philippe's is the consciousness most often penetrated by the narrator, but Vinca is the character that is more habitually and specifically identified with the natural elements. Eyes, hair, movements, clothes are constantly signalled in a complex sequence of interrelated references, in which the androgynous dominates. Vinca is spare and swift; she is child, boy, animal, sea-nymph, Diana-figure. A recurrent image is of her running, leaping, balancing, swimming; she throws pebbles hard and straight, she can carry Philippe on her back. She moves with 'une célérité anguleuse' (p.95), and hers is the 'jambe de bête fine, faite pour la course et le saut' (p.94), with 'durs genoux ciselés finement' (p.110). Her hair links her directly to the book's title; its colour and its texture however suggest harvest rather than the corn in its greenness. But a playful tone stresses its sun-bleached roughness — 'deux courts balais couleur de blé' (p.44), 'paille raide et bien dorée' (p.32), and only sometimes does 'le chaume soyeux' (p.173) link more sensuously to the threshed buckwheat of the book's climax.

It is Vinca's eyes that are most frequently described or referred to: of a vivid rich blue, they characterise her intimately through the implications of her Christian name (the periwinkle) and they are used to convey her moods and emotions, her charm and her directness. Their main linguistic correspondents are water and flowers, with an emphasis on the play of light. These eyes gleam, blaze and shimmer. The 'bleu incomparable de ses yeux' (p.110) can be 'bleu de pervenche' (p.170) or 'bleu de flamme' (p.159). It is like the 'pluie printanière' (p.31), like 'eau fraîche' (p.110), and in a final triumphant notation 'les yeux de Vinca luttaient d'azur avec la mer matinale' (p.187). The many 'pervenche' references are paralleled by less direct but pervasive ones to the sea holly: '... cette combe ronde, tapissée de chardons de dune, combe qu'à cause de la couleur des chardons bleus on nommait "les Yeux de Vinca"' (p.137). By such an identification and christening is Vinca given sway over the familiar scene. Yet the tribute is subverted since these are the very thistles that Phil picks and bundles up and throws so unceremoniously over Mme Dalleray's wall. But another link with Vinca is also established through her clothes; notably her 'fishing hat', 'ce béret de laine hérissé et bleuâtre comme un chardon des dunes' (p.31), that reappears a little later as 'un béret de laine bleue, décoloré comme un chardon des dunes' (p.51) in marked contrast to the elegance of the 'dame tout de blanc vêtue' (p.52). Vinca also has a 'robe bleue couleur de chardon bleu' (p.130), and another (or possibly the same one?) that is the colour of her eyes (pp.44, 115). The whites of her eyes gleam too, like mother-of-pearl and moonlight (pp.154, 170). The water and flower images are linked simply in the first lines of the book 'la Pervenche, Vinca aux yeux couleur de pluie printanière' (p.31) but much more profoundly and significantly when her absence is evoked and Phil cannot find her: '... deux yeux bleus, riches de deux ou trois bleus et d'un peu de mauve, ne fleurirent nulle part pour désaltérer les siens' (p.131). So a distinctive quality is established, more than the effect of youth and freshness, firm, constant, vulnerable, with the promise of sustenance, fruition.

Vinca is defined too, through her clothes, often blue and white, with touches of pink and green. Shrimping is ritualised by the shabby clothes, the blue and green skirt, the blue beret, that link her to her childhood. In contrast, a best dress of white starched and flounced organdie makes Phil uneasy ('dimanche à Tahiti' he jeers, p.39); she is distanced from the world of Nature and is drawn into the conventions of adulthood. But this same dress is crushed and soiled when Vinca rushes out to comfort Phil in the darkness. White, however, can also be part of the clothes of a freer Vinca, and the colours that reflect sky, sea, grass and flowers. The dominant blue ('sweater bleu', p.68; 'bandelette bleue', p.69; 'robe de crépon bleu', p.115), already present on the first page, is worn by Vinca ('mon Kimono bleu', p.177) when she joins Phil at night outside and draws him to make love to her. Offord, in a study of colour symbolism (*37*), wants us to make further and closer psychological identifications, Vinca's sewing of a pink frill on to her blue dress with nascent sexuality, for instance, and green with her jealousy. One disconcerting image of Vinca shows her as 'enfant en sarrau violâtre décoloré aux épaules' (p.132), obsessively and angrily absorbed in her monotonous domestic tasks, shutting out a puzzled, wary Phil.

If Vinca's emotions are not often analysed in depth, her manner, appearance and reactions are meticulously conveyed, and the shifting moods and stances emerge almost as multiple personalities through the variety of noun-groupings which characterise her. Male, female, adult, child, animal, all these categories define her. The most explicit image of her ambivalence is not of alternating selves but of a divided being:

> Une amante, de tout blessée, assez magnifique pour tout pardonner, resplendissait dans le haut du visage de Vinca; une petite fille désolée, un peu comique, grimaçait gentiment par sa bouche et son menton tremblant. (p.162)

Elsewhere she is boy-like: 'une sérénité de petit garçon' (p.32), 'un collégien déguisé' (p.55), 'un jeune échanson' (p.69). A number of female roles and identities are deployed: 'une sagesse de femme' (pp.47-48), 'la petite idole' (p.42), 'son bon sens habituel de petite

bourgeoise' (p.61), 'sa besogne de petite squaw' (p.70), 'cette jeune
ménagère coiffée à la Jeanne d'Arc' (p.133). The animal images
stress a lithe freedom of movement, and often consolidate a sense of
androgyny. Vinca swims 'comme un petit phoque' (p.37) when she
and Phil relax into child-like play; her 'jambe de bête fine, faite pour
la course et le saut' (p.94) does not arouse desire but 'l'espèce
d'exaltation que l'on voue à un style pur'. At such a time Vinca seems
a Diana. She is also the Chloe to Phil's Daphnis (p.61), and the pear
that she bites into in the dark garden recalls Persephone, poised
between two worlds, the dangerous pomegranate in her hand. But a
harsher deity stands over a sobbing Phil, her blood-stained fish-spear
in her hand, stiffened by 'un mépris, tout viril' (p.114). Vinca is a
flower of Nature, the periwinkle; she is both victor and enchained[1]
(*46*, p.128). But the final image of her is enigmatic: 'cette petite fille
neuve' (p.188).

Philippe

Philippe Audebert is different from other adolescents in Colette's
fiction because of the effect on him of the familiar comradeship with
Vinca and his certainty that he loves her. Tenderness, warmth,
reliance, protectiveness, patronage, touches of romantic idealism
accompany a growing sexual awareness, and Philippe is unusually
sensitised to quite subtle emotions. His attachment is talismanic.
'L'amour, grandi avant eux, avait enchanté leur enfance et gardé leur
adolescence des amitiés équivoques' (p.61). Yet his understanding of
feminine psychology is awkward and rudimentary and he refers to
his novel-reading for clues, baffled by Vinca's moods, nonplussed by
Camille's style.

He is apparently more introspective than Vinca, and through
him come the moments of exquisite awareness of mutability, of the
quality of experience, accessible through the dreamy passivity that
he often sinks into. Here he is closest to the Alain of *La Chatte*. But
he is also the limited, inexperienced and not over-intelligent
bourgeois, 'enfant d'un petit industriel parisien' (p.47). He is further

[1]Derivations from the Latin *vincere* 'to conquer'.

defined as he relates to Colette's general image of the male, 'né pour
la chasse et la tromperie' (p.32), 'un homme exigeant, héritier
âprement résolu à jouir des biens que lui destinent le temps et les lois
humaines' (p.63).

The oscillation between childish and adult identities patterns
the novel, and is accentuated because it is exteriorised through Mme
Dalleray's perceptions and words. She moves from 'Hep! petit!' to a
half-ironic 'Monsieur' at their first meeting, but she is a woman who
will always want to make her own terms. She has to take pains to
seduce him: he is no easy victim, protected as he is by his tie with
Vinca, but 'un antagoniste ébloui et circonspect' (p.98).

This seduction is remembered by him as a sensual kaleido-
scope, 'des saillies lumineuses qui se hissaient au jour et y prenaient
la couleur de l'or, de la chair, l'éclat d'un œil mouillé, d'une bague ou
d'un ongle' (p.109). His reaction, on his return, is to burst into tears,
or to seek the doubtful comfort of a cantankerous dog. A later
uncontrollable outburst of tears alerts Vinca to his altered state. 'On
assure qu'elles pleurent après' (p.184) is the received wisdom of his
age-group about girls. In fact, Vinca's moments of weakness, her
tears, her passive slide towards possible suicide, take place before
her physical union with Phil; her retreat to the sofa can be construed
as a response to a natural event, a menstrual lassitude. The wake of
Phil's dizzying relationship with Camille is however a more startling
physical enfeeblement; he faints, and takes to his bed. 'Ce convales-
cent du plaisir' (p.117) relishes the 'suavité de la défaite' (p.106); his
physique and his whole being are seen to lurch towards the feminine
— 'des traits plaintifs, et moins pareils à ceux d'un homme qu'à ceux
d'une jeune fille meurtrie' (p.107).

At sixteen and a half Philippe judges himself discontentedly to
be 'à peu près homme, à peu près libre, à peu près amoureux' (p.47).
But the novel seeks to persuade us that these are the most vivid and
devastating experiences that he is ever likely to have. His dark charm
will settle to an even banality, his sensitivity be blunted. Yet now he
is distinguished by emotions that he cannot fully appreciate,
'enfermé dans son précoce amour comme un prince orphelin dans un
palais trop vaste' (p.80).

Madame Dalleray

'La dame en blanc', 'Elle', 'Mme Dalleray' — Philippe continues to think of his 'maître' in these terms even after their erotic encounters, rather than using 'le prénom insexué' Camille (p.125). When she first walks up to him Phil is prone among the dunes, and at their second meeting, outside her villa Ker-Anna, he is again half-clothed, again sprawled flat. The dominance of the 'génie spoliateur' (p.106), the 'belle démone autoritaire' (p.121), reinforced by the ironic and distancing condescension of her address, could not be more clearly signalled. Like the two families she is Parisian, but here on the coast she manifests no response to the natural elements. Her elegance is out of place as her high heels sink in the sand, and the ambiance with which she is at ease is the cool, dark interior of her house, crowded with cushions, perfumed, offering exotic fruits and bitter drinks, its erotic charge concentrated by the narrator on to the plumage of her parrot. 'Un ara rouge et bleu, sur son perchoir, ouvrit son aile avec un bruit d'éventail, pour montrer son aisselle couleur de chair émue' (pp.83-84) (later 'comme la chair des pêches', p.88).

We see Mme Dalleray through Phil's eyes, for the most part, and have no direct access to her thinking. To him she is inscrutable, a kind of aloof but disturbing exotic deity, with her gleaming black hair and creamy complexion. Her strategy is a wary stillness, her words are casual or enigmatic. Meanwhile, Phil is inarticulate and clumsy, as panic and bravado struggle in his mind. So there is a subtext to their dialogue, explicit in the case of Phil, implicit for Mme Dalleray. The underlying melancholy of her situation, her isolation, and even her vulnerability, emerge when Phil, grown more complacent, assumes that he will be welcome to visit her in Paris at snatched moments between lectures. 'Une petite contraction pénible' (p.127) reminds her that she is able to feel pain, we see her contemplating Phil dispassionately and regretfully, and soon afterwards she leaves Brittany.

Some critics have found the figure of Mme Dalleray exaggerated and artificial, and A. Bazin in praising Edwige Feuillère's performance in the film of 1954 considers it a more appropriate or realistic portrayal of the 'older woman' (*16*). But, as we have seen, everything to do with Mme Dalleray is angled through Philippe's consciousness, and he, disconcerted and dazzled, is unable to reconcile this experience with anything else in his life. It is the 'somptueux cauchemar' (p.84) to which his body adjusts hesitantly and then luxuriously, but which to his mind remains a separate world. If the rich Eastern fabrics, the hangings, the 'chair rouge du melon' (p.99) can seem the rather obvious props of a 1920s *femme fatale*, they also delimit figuratively a closed world whose 'coloris brûlant et faux' (p.88) is deliberately set against the bright freshness of Nature and the figure of Vinca.

Narrative voice

Unlike the mode of most of the other third-person fictional texts, the voice of the narrator intervenes fairly often in *Le Blé en herbe* to comment and annotate for the reader. Because of the scrupulous autonomy that Colette gives to all of the dialogue and much of the *style indirect libre* material, this voice is not unduly intrusive, but it does set up, from early on, a habit of generalisation whose aim, it would seem, is to balance the uniqueness of the individual with the predestination implied by strong gender, class and group affiliations. Individuals are inserted into a non-historical continuum where their actions conform, often semi-consciously, to a pre-determined pattern. Colette appears to be setting out to enhance the experience of the adolescents by this means, deepening or extending its significance beyond their own hesitant self-awareness. There are a number of comments of the 'like all males/females' type, and these could easily have become heavy-handed, were it not for the virtuoso techniques of gender subversion that are deployed. These are often couched in negative constructions, pointing up limitations in the characters' understanding:

> Il méconnaissait, hargneux, la mission de durer, dévolue
> à toutes les espèces femelles. (p.163)

> Il n'imaginait pas qu'un plaisir mal donné, mal reçu est
> une œuvre perfectible. (p.185)

Sometimes this immaturity seems to be condoned as being the concomitant of a childish absolutism and idealism that is accorded a form of moral value: 'la dignité revêche des enfants' (p.33); 'car les amants de seize ans n'admettent ni le changement, ni la maladie, ni l'infidélité' (p.67). But the process of ageing will inevitably weaken and marginalise such attitudes. Meanwhile Colette feels it to be appropriate for the narrator to interpret overtly a *moment privilégié* of Phil's.

> Philippe ne sut pas se dire: "Il est peu d'heures dans la
> vie où le corps content, les yeux récompensés et le cœur
> léger, retentissant, presque vide, reçoivent en un moment
> tout ce qu'ils peuvent contenir, et je me souviendrai de
> celle-ci"; mais il suffit pourtant d'une clarine fêlée et de
> la voix du chevreau qui la balançait à son cou, pour que
> les coins de sa bouche tressaillissent d'angoisse, et que le
> plaisir emplît ses yeux de larmes. (p.52)

The reader may feel that this notation could well stand on its own, without the alternative verbalisation. Still more, perhaps, will the reader baulk at the proleptic sentence of the final paragraph that emphasises Phil's bewildered and disillusioned reaction to his sighting of an apparently relaxed and serene Vinca, but also breaks through the artistic unity of the expression of that reaction: 'Il ne songea pas non plus que dans quelques semaines l'enfant qui chantait pouvait pleurer, effarée, condamnée, à la même fenêtre' (p.188). Yet the narrator's reticence at this point does by comparison disconcert, and leave the way open to a large variety of interpretations, much more so than elsewhere in the text.

The end of *Le Blé en herbe* caused Colette a great deal of trouble. She writes to Marguerite Moreno:

> J'ai fini — que je crois — "Le Seuil". Non sans
> tourments! La dernière page, exactement, m'a coûté
> toute ma première journée de Castel-Novel, — et je te
> défie bien, en le lisant, de t'en douter. Quoi, ces vingt
> lignes où il y a ni cabuchon ni ciselure ... Hélas, c'est
> comme ça. C'est la *proportion* qui m'a donné du mal. J'ai
> une telle horreur de la grandiloquence finale. (*12*, p.65)

This extract also helps, incidentally, to dispel two widely-held
beliefs about Colette's writing habits, one that she tossed off her
chapters with nonchalant ease, the other that she needed to be on the
site of her fictional settings to compose them.

From the beginning many commentators identified very
positively with Vinca's initiative in turning the tables on Mme
Dalleray and provoking Phil into making love to her. Larnac writes
in 1927: 'Alors, dans un élan quasi-maternel, la petite Vinca se livre
à celui qu'elle aime, pour le sauver' (*31*, p.153). He is identifying
generosity as her prime motivation, and this deflects attention from
the rather harsher reaction of wounded pride and resolution to which
jealousy prompts her. Ward Jouve is nearer the mark when she says
'Vinca reconquers Philippe. In her strange prescient power and
endurance, in her ability to go for what she wants, she is the equal of
the lady-in-white' (*46*, p.129). Vinca is aware, too, of the presence of
the erotic; but in Beauvoir's view her final serenity is the result of a
décalage that she finds common in young girls between attraction
and erotic response.

> C'est qu'elle ne s'est pas sentie "possédée", elle a mis au
> contraire son orgueil à se délivrer de sa virginité, elle n'a
> pas éprouvé d'égarement bouleversant; en vérité, Phil a
> tort de s'étonner, son amie n'a pas connu le mâle.
> (*Le Deuxième Sexe*, 1949, I, p.460)

Since the final pages are filtered through Phil's consciousness we can
feel closer to his anxious disillusion. But it remains difficult to
predict his subsequent reactions. He has reared away in panic at

Vinca's attempt to discuss openly his affair with Mme Dalleray, and he can only bring himself to project an image of a drooping and devastated girl, an image that is smartly challenged by the real Vinca with her healthy fuchsia. However, in a provocative sally Angela Carter ascribes his disarray to a different source altogether.

> The beautiful ... lady who seduces him, whom he calls his 'master', is not really Vinca's rival at all, but her fellow conspirator in the ugly plot to 'make a man' of Phil with all that implies of futility and arrogance and complacency. (22, p.178)

She sees Colette's men as distorted and destroyed by love, and then resented and rejected by their partners: 'Kiss Prince Charming and he instantly turns into a frog', she comments tartly.

Technique

There is however one area of Colette's writing which has not given rise to any controversy, and that is her use of images of the sea-shore that weave in and out of the thematic text, extending and qualifying the characters' experience. The allusions are marked by a constant but not intrusive particularity. Flowers, birds, fish, trees, all are named. Oregano and thyme, melilot and sea-holly add their distinctive presence to the sea in its various manifestations, 'La mer déserte, d'un bleu noir d'hirondelle' (p.115), 'un doux temps breton qui voilait de brume la terre et mêlait à la mer un lait immatériel' (p.89). The sea is that subtle and vigorous sustaining element that Michelet describes as 'la mer de lait' and 'la fleur de sang', and 'cette grande force, salutaire, mais âpre' (*La Mer*, Folio, 1983, pp.114, 278). The adolescents' daily bathe is their most cherished link with their childhood; but the sea is also the element into which each at one point in the text thinks of slipping forever in a moment of passive but dramatised despair. Its ebb and flow parallel all the anguish and gaiety of these crucial weeks.

There are no sustained set-pieces of description in this novel, none of the close, intense focus that marks Colette's 'sea-shore' pieces, 'Regarde' and 'La Flaque' (*4*, pp.194, 196), where the margins of this Atlantic ocean are brought to life in all the colour and variety of their flora and fauna. What we do have are memorable glimpses and sensations that form an unobtrusive continuum within which words, actions and emotions are harmonised or set in relief. It is easy to select 'le chuchotement humide d'une poignée de crevettes' (p.51) or 'une petite vague exténuée, qui claquait faiblement comme un linge mouillé' (p.103). But it is important to recognise how closely such notations are meshed into the general texture and how they provide one term of the interaction of person and milieu. 'Elle retrouva, avec un ravissement indigné, le rayon du couchant dans les yeux noirs de Philippe' (p.64) is the form of Vinca's painful suspicion. And Philippe's own melancholic and regressive lethargy is linked not just to 'grass', but to something more specific and delicately perceived: 'Il essuya le sable de ses mains à une touffe de serpolet mouillé, chargée de fleurs et de petits frelons saisis par la pluie, qui attendaient, engourdis, le prochain rayon' (p.58). The Vinca that he watches at this moment is seen in one of Colette's sinuous art-nouveau images: 'Mais il regarda contre la vitre, entre les longues larmes de la pluie et les corolles tournoyantes des volubilis défaits, le visage de Vinca...' (p.59).

This latter is, too, one of the pairs or series of images that echo through the text. Vinca is again at a window in the last pages, under a quite different sky. The saucer that Philippe smashes as he breaks away from Mme Dalleray's touch (p.99) is matched by the slate that crashes down at his feet during the squalls of early autumn (p.130). The two curlews that fly over as he lies in the sea become the poignant reminder of a lost state.

> Un petit nuage couvrant le soleil haut, Phil ouvrit les yeux et vit passer au-dessus de lui les ventres ombrés, les grands becs effilés et les pattes sombres, repliées en plein vol, d'un couple de courlis. (p.39)

> Un couple de courlis passa au-dessus de Philippe, assez
> bas pour qu'il entendît le cri de voilure de leurs ailes
> tendues, et leur piaulement sur la mer plongea, dans la
> mémoire ouverte et sans défense de l'adolescent,
> jusqu'au fond de quinze années pures, suspendues à un
> rivage blond, à une enfant qui à ses côtés grandissait,
> portant sa tête blonde et droite comme un épi. (p.105)

Here the sea images and sounds, sky, land and feminine presence are
meshed in with the central metaphor of the title, the upright corn and
its metamorphosis.

One reason for the patterns of repetition in the novel, the series
of almost lyrical recalls, was the necessity, in the original episodic
publication, to plant identification tags for the reader.[2] But they do
not interrupt the flow of the text, and are paralleled by other linguistic systems that operate throughout. A military lexicon is applied in
situations that are seen as attack, defence, defeat, sally. The more
continuous use of the terminology of illness and violence: weakness,
fainting, bruising, beating, death, operates on several planes and
describes actual scratches, blows and struggles while referring
metaphorically to emotional hurts and psychological eclipses of
vitality.

Many of the effects, then, are allusive rather than explicit; the
tone is unemphatic but never frivolous, sympathetic but not didactic
or intense. A warning voice speaks to us sometimes, telling us that
this is 'le monde des émotions qu'on nomme, à la légère, physiques'
(p.133), emphasising one of the text's many paradoxes, another of
which is the play between the ordinary and the unique that charac-
terises these adolescents at this moment of their experience. 'Because
of their age, because of their passion, Vinca and Philippe rise, like
small deities, above their environment; they are in a temporary state
of grace' (*34*, p.145).

---

[2] Details of their titles and dates are ably and fully discussed in their different
editions by the editors B. Stimpson and C. Pichois; v. appendix.

4. La Chatte

When Colette published *La Chatte* in 1933, she was sixty. It was one of a series of third-person narrator novels that appeared between 1920 and 1942 and that exhibit a sure control over this medium. The novels that precede and follow it, *La Seconde* and *Duo*, concern couples who have been married for some years, but in *La Chatte* the period just before and after the marriage of a young bourgeois couple is explored. This may recall the structure of *Chéri*, where the young man's union with Edmée is overshadowed by the figure of Léa. Here in *La Chatte*, however, Alain's pre-existing attachment is to his cat.

In 1933 Colette's life might have been seen as a fairly settled one. For some time she had owned La Treille Muscate, her modest house near Saint-Tropez, she lived in a suite at the Claridge Hotel in Paris, and her relationship with Maurice Goudeket was firmly established; they were to marry in 1935. But her temperament and the financial stringencies of that period stimulated her to a remarkable and often impetuous round of activity. To a ground-base of dramatic criticism must be added lecture-tours, film-dialogues, journalism of various types, as well as the 1932 commercial venture, her short-lived beauty salon. Somehow Colette also managed to write some of her most elaborate, mature and penetrating personal documents, from the openly referential *Mes apprentissages* of 1936 to the imaginative recall of her mother in *Sido* (1930), the collected sketches of *Prisons et paradis* (1932), and the ambitious, original, exploratory fictions of *La Naissance du jour* (1928) and *Ces plaisirs* (1932, later called *Le Pur et l'impur*). Compared with these two latter works, where a 'Colette' figure pursues a complex and vividly-dramatised meditation on the nature of sexual love and individual fulfilment, *La Chatte* does not offer any striking technical innovations or psychological surprises. But this does not mean that it caused no stir on its appearance, or that it has not set off controversy ever since.

By this time Colette's style had become synonymous with grace and poise, and was often identified with what were seen as peculiarly French qualities of economy and control. It would have been a brave critic who would have directly assaulted these. But this did not shield the works from a different kind of attack, entailing the dissociation of content and form. It is interesting that this tactic extended to Anglo-Saxon critics; the *TLS* reviewer of a 1953 translation does not mince words: '"The Cat" is a brilliant piece of writing but it is a vile story' (16 October), and a contemporary reviewer had dismissed the novel in similar terms, but because of its slightness: 'Having read the book with delight, on account of the beauty of the writing, we doubt if we shall open it again because there is so little in it' (*TLS*, 10 August, 1933).

So what is this slight and perhaps disturbing story? During a few weeks of late spring and early summer in Paris, at a time that seems contemporary with the writing of the novel, the marriage of Alain and Camille takes them to temporary quarters in a friend's elevated and very modern flat while they await the completion of the extension that is being built for them to Alain's family house. Tensions in their relationship come to focus upon Alain's cat Saha who joins them in the flat, and whom Camille tries to kill by pushing her off the balcony. Alain retreats to his home with the uninjured animal; a fresh start for the marriage seems unlikely.

It is of course the role of the cat that creates uncertainty and unease in the mind of the reader, or rather the powerful emotional, sensual and imaginative hold that Saha has upon Alain's consciousness, a hold that proves incompatible with attraction to a young human. The narrator does not evaluate these relationships, which Alain considers different in quality but not perhaps in kind; again, the narrator does not overtly dispute this assumption. 'Tu me sacrifies à une bête! Je suis ta femme, tout de même! Tu me laisses pour une bête!' (p.155), exclaims Camille, angry and incredulous. Marriages have foundered for much less reason than this. But the presence of Saha is no manufactured excuse; her identity is bound up intimately with all levels of Alain's self-image.

What the reader can easily perceive, however, is the marked pattern of contrasts in the structure of the text. There are simple dichotomies between Alain's graceful blond langour and the decisive, energetic brunette Camille, between the Amparats' old-established discreet traditions in the silk-trade and the bustling commercialism of Camille's family firm of washing-machine manufacturers, between the large, comfortable house and garden in Neuilly and the uncompromising 'quart de Brie' apartment, with its wedge-shaped rooms and bare white walls. But a more complicated patterning has been identified by those critics who see the text in terms of a series of triads: a *ménage à trois*, three locales (including the half-built extension), the nine storeys of the apartment-block, three terraces, three poplars, three-walled rooms, the three-month period, the three-year-old cat. This allows for a more complex interaction between elements, more shading-off of interpretations.

Camille

The young girl of nineteen who marries Alain is never seen in her own domestic context, and although her parents, the Malmert couple, are present in the first scene, they hardly emerge as individuals. They are indulgent and gently reproving, but there is almost nothing to sketch in a family relationship. Camille seems to emerge new-minted from her comfortable milieu, and this seems consonant with her confident response to the present, her orientation towards the future.

Camille is perceived almost wholly through Alain's consciousness: he is the 'focaliser', to use Genette's term. Only in one scene is she separate from him. Slim, dark, lively, vivid, clean-drawn, immaculately made-up and dressed, she has a smooth and glistening smartness. Alain admires the way she is turned out, and concedes that others see them as a 'joli couple' (p.97). She is often seen in the white that suits her: '... il fut tout au spectacle de Camille en blanc, un petit pinceau noir de cheveux bien taillés sur les tempes, une mince cravate rouge au cou, et le même rouge sur sa bouche' (p.39), 'Elle était jolie tous les soirs à la même heure, en pyjama blanc' (p.69). Hers is never an unobtrusive presence, and it is often conveyed in hard, shining, unyielding allusions. Alain looks back to 'une fillette très brune, dont les larges yeux et les cheveux noirs en rouleaux rivalisaient d'éclat hostile et minéral' (p.34), and now he reflects that 'le brillant de ses yeux s'accorde avec des cheveux propres, lavés souvent, gommés, et couleur de piano neuf' (p.10).

This is a young girl who smokes, drives fast, and sometimes swears. Alain chides her for her ungrammatical speech. His mother tries hard to be impartial, but at a moment of crisis concedes that 'Elle n'est pas si mauvaise, cette petite Malmert. Un peu... grosse, un peu sans manières' (p.148). The hostility of the old family servants, however, is gleeful and overt. They refer to her loud voice, her assertiveness, and see her as a predator upon their master, an intruder into their domain, whom they can only fight with derision. It is as though they can hear her mocking of them as 'Quel musée!' (p.71).

But it is the attitude of Saha to her that consolidates the sense of Camille's isolation. In the Amparat garden she is a visitor still, and any familiarity on her part provokes a panic reaction in Alain, 'Pas ici, pas ici — pas encore' (p.61). But here Saha can withdraw into seclusion; not so in the starkness of the flat, where indifference is no longer possible. The cat's new routines can only protect her for so long against the devastating pressures of heroic tolerance and contained aversion. Saha's reactions are charted meticulously and delicately, and they are a significant contribution to impressions of Camille, even before the overt and sinister duel between these females.

Most crucial of all, inevitably, is Alain's attitude. He accepts what is tantamount to an arranged marriage passively and even complacently, he seldom speaks unpleasantly or sharply to his wife, but the form of the text reveals the undercurrents of rivalry, pique and resentment, the childish scoring of points, the apprehension, the withdrawal that flood through his emotional being. It is the physical identity of Camille that provokes these reactions. The crux of the matter is the contrast between her darkness and his fairness. This is used to point up the alienness of each, and especially of Camille for Alain: 'il s'ébahit, jusqu'au scandale, de comprendre combien Camille était brune' (p.82). Meanwhile, Camille views her fiancé admiringly: 'C'est fou d'être blond à ce point là!' (p.13). She is indulgent, amused, attracted. His reactions are less candid, more complex and oblique. He is directly disgusted by the black hairs in the washbasin, 'La vue d'un fin cheveu très noir, collé au bord d'une cuvette, lui donna la nausée' (p.83); he is so disturbed by her wide-open dark eyes that he even reduces their circumference in the photographs that he owns (p.28), and he notes his own preference for her elongated shadow upon the wall. 'Qu'elle est belle sur le mur! Juste assez étirée, juste comme je l'aimerais...' (p.14).

Hers is not a voluptuous body, but it imposes itself insistently. In the kind of sense-effects that Colette developed boldly, the smell of her body is emphasised, through a profusion of vegetative images. Her 'vigoureuse odeur de brune' clings to the 'algue' (p.43) of her body-hair: 'Echauffée, l'étrangère fleurait le bois mordu par la flamme, le bouleau, la violette, tout un bouquet de douces odeurs sombres et tenaces, qui demeuraient longtemps attachées aux paumes' (p.84). But these smells do not make a direct appeal to Alain's sensuality: ' — Tu es comme l'odeur des roses, dit-il un jour à Camille, tu ôtes l'appétit' (p.84).

While they were engaged, Alain never touched or saw her body directly. The slim legs, that he considers to be her best feature, are always stockinged. She is frank, but modest. We see her nudity suddenly, as he awakens on the day after his wedding. Alain is attracted, intrigued, shocked and repelled all at once while he watches a self-confident, relaxed naked girl sit at the dressing-table as she smokes a cigarette, and greet him unselfconsciously. Her easy manner and her lack of physical shame seem like effrontery to him; they upset all the conventions which he has absorbed about his role as sexual initiator and hers as timid, passive and grateful disciple. He struggles to maintain supremacy, by class-inspired strictures: 'Elle a le dos peuple' (p.42).

The couple achieve a reasonable sexual equilibrium, but the disturbance of roles continues, with Camille often starting their love-making and undressing her husband, while Alain can take a perverse pleasure in humiliating and thwarting his wife by avoiding physical contact with her. He is confused by the fear and aversion that he feels for what Stewart calls her 'corporeal darkness' (*44*, p.70); this mirrors and challenges some element of his own psyche with which he cannot come to terms. He clutches gratefully at a moral dimension of Camille's sexuality, 'il respecta cette discrétion et cette fierté' (p.48), and his defences fall when he can perceive her, unusually, as either cat-like — 'Elle gisait contre lui, bras et jambes mollement pliés, les mains à demi fermées et féline pour la première fois' (p.48) — or boyish, 'une grâce si garçonnière et si fraternelle qu'il faillit se réfugier sur son épaule' (p.17). This physical response of burying the head in the neck or shoulder of the partner, so frequent with Chéri and Léa, is identified by Resch as Colette's characteristic representation of the male seeking comfort and nurture, and when Alain returns to his family home he embraces his mother, seeking her neck tearfully in just such a gesture.

But for the most part the relationship is easy-going on the surface, adversarial below it. In a text called 'Nudité' (1943) Colette reflected on attitudes to female nakedness through reminiscences of music-hall experience and apparently factually-based anecdotes, one of which recounts the estrangement of a young couple. The husband eventually confesses to 'Colette' that his wedding-night lecture on the naturalness of nudity resulted almost immediately in a fearless and easy display of her body outside the bed by his spouse, and that he is now unable to conceal his hurt and aversion. The Colette-narrator of this text sympathises with, or at least recognises, the feelings of the male — 'ô toi ombrageuse, renaissante et délicate pudeur de l'homme' (*5*, VIII, p.449) — and hopes that an instinctual reserve and modesty may eventually make its appearance in the girl. Colette often suggests that a deeper and more complex understanding of passion will bring reserve, self-doubt, apprehension, while over-confident nudity can betoken shallowness or ignorance. For the older woman of Colette's fiction, for Léa or for the Marco of 'Le Képi', who exuberantly dons her lover's military cap, it can spell disaster. Here, however, Camille's sensuality is not seen as insensitive, and

Alain's rejection of her cannot be construed as her fault. She represents one identification of the 'natural'; Saha represents another.

But a harsher view of Camille has often been taken by critics. She does, after all, attempt to murder the cat, and her subsequent reactions do not seem to include remorse. For most people this is disturbing, for some it will be unforgivable. Beaumont believes that she is speaking for Colette when she says 'La maudite, c'est celle qui a essayé de tuer la Chatte' (*17*, p.30), but the text is more ambivalent than this, and because the struggle is presented as a series of inter-related movements and the narrator does not probe into the woman's motivation, see into her mind, there is no moral context: the actions emerge, sharp-cut, and seem both unplanned and inevitable.

When critics have tried for a typology of Colette's women characters Camille has tended to emerge in a negative category. From Marks onwards Vinca will be seen as the warm, sensitive, giving younger woman, Camille, with her bisexual fore-name, as hard, unreflective, brittle. But this is to underestimate how consistently Camille is seen through Alain's consciousness. And in any case she could hardly be called brash. As she chatters to her parents in the first scene we see her moderate her vocabulary to suit their conventions; later she corrects herself to please Alain. But it is in her attitude to her new relationship that she is at her most sensitive. She softens, seeks to please, watches Alain's moods. 'Elle s'appuyait à son bras, un peu molle, incertaine exceptionnellement' (p.60). Alone with Saha, she reverts to a harder, more self-sufficient persona.

> Dès que Camille était seule, elle ressemblait beaucoup à la petite fille qui ne voulait pas dire bonjour, et son visage retournait à l'enfance par l'expression de naïveté inhumaine, d'angélique dureté qui ennoblit les visages enfantins. (pp.111-12)

This is the self which is the aggressor, the destroyer, and in the duel with Saha all hint of vulgarity falls away. She is intent, concentrated, a pure force.

Camille is a lonely figure. She has no friends, no confidant, no faith in comradeship: 'les jeunes filles, expliqua-t-elle assez amèrement, les jeunes filles, tu sais, ça ne tient pas honnêtement ensemble... Ça n'a pas de solidarité' (p.72). This perception sensitises her to the disloyalty that she identifies as a key factor in Alain's rejection of her. 'Enfin, tu es si peu de mon parti' (p.153). When Alain leaves her, she reappears, putting on a brave front, wearing her new suit; she is prepared to be conciliatory, makes advances. Alain is hostile to this approach: 'Déjà elle organise, déjà elle jette des fils de trame, des passerelles, déjà elle ramasse, recoud, retisse ... C'est terrible' (p.158). Yet this is exactly the female faculty that Colette often puts forward for approval. The ability to survive is identified by her as the female prerogative, an ability which makes the woman often stronger than the man. Edmée makes a new life for herself, while still living in the same house as an alienated Chéri; Renée, of *La Vagabonde*, settles for self-sufficiency and her theatrical career. Colette's distinction is to show her heroines in a low-key process of make-do and mend, in which the paralysing intensity of grief, loneliness, yearning is dispelled and exorcised by patterns of domestic and personal activity: concern with clothes, grooming, food, flowers. To maintain their self-respect characters like Julie de Carneilhan and the Alice of *Duo* retreat to the milieux of their adolescence, where they can renew their sense of identity. Camille, however, makes no attempt to return to her family, even though she has been married for only a few weeks. She plans to go to friends in Brittany, taking the 'roadster'. Like many of Colette's female figures, she takes a modest step into the future, drawing on reserves of resilience, endurance and self-respect.

Alain

Rituals dominate Alain's life. As he breakfasts with Saha, he imagines Camille's itinerant and casual snack.

> Elle mord à même une lame de jambon maigre, serrée entre deux biscottes, et dans une pomme d'Amérique. Et

> elle pose et oublie, de meuble en meuble, une tasse de
> thé sans sucre... (p.30)

He is the more comforted by his custom-hallowed meal of bread and
honey with milky coffee, and it offers one of the moments that link
him overtly with his boyhood.

> Enfin un tout petit Alain, dissimulé au fond d'un grand
> garçon blond et beau, attendait impatient que la fin du
> déjeuner lui permît de lécher en tous sens la cuiller du
> pot à miel, une vieille cuiller d'ivoire noircie et
> cartilagineuse. (pp.29-30)

Although she is only three years old, Saha has been wholly assimi-
lated into these solipsistic and regressive conventions, and she
enhances and extends them by her sensitive acquiescence. Alain is
repeatedly defined by the narrator by reference to his previous
identities in time; he returns to the garden of the morning after his
wedding 'en adolescent qui a découché' (p.53), sleep returns him to
his 'enfance délicate et mal dirigée' (p.23). His mother's response to
his fantasies or his egotism is 'quel enfant' (p.147, cf. p.91). The
elderly servants obviously see him as the child of the household, and
the manager of the family silk firm blocks any of his suggestions
with a patronising amusement. Camille mocks him, 'Comme tu es
dix-huit cent trente' (p.84), suggesting that these are the 1930s, not
the 1830s. There is nothing to break this continuum until his
marriage, and this event sharpens his own consciousness of just how
deeply his identity is bound up with this seamless projection of past
into present, externalised in the vegetative correlatives of the garden.
It is these that represent Alain's childhood to him, as his inner gaze
modifies the proportions of the trees; they swell above him as his
stature shrinks, and lost features of the garden rise up with Proustian
clarity (p.32).

Alain's narcissism turns firstly on his physical appearance, and
is often conveyed through the mirrors that are such a typical motif of
Colette's. He lingers complacently in the glass-panelled bathroom of

the flat. In a haunting image he watches Saha watching him in the mirror at home. He sees his own blondness as a necessary condition of his identity, not the complement of darkness, but its obverse. 'Brun, je serais affreux' (pp.20-21) he comments, with startling prescience, given his ambivalence towards Camille. Meanwhile, Camille's admiring gaze centres more than once on Alain's grey-green eyes, with their dark lashes.

But it is the emotional narcissism that dominates the text. His own reflections, constantly conveyed by the narrator, sometimes in direct but unvoiced speech, more often in long swirls of reverie, or in the acid, defensive sub-text that accompanies his bland, neutral dialogues with Camille, create the main discourse of the novel. They circle round, tenacious but undirected, and seem to absorb all his energies. His physical person is passive, lethargic. 'Mollement' is the adverb that is several times applied to his movements. He is at ease in the darkness, and sleep is another cherished ritual, so much so that sharing a bed with Camille represents not enrichment but deprivation. A whole dimension of the text represents this imaginative and dream state. Yet the experience has its sinister side. It is 'son naufrage quotidien' (p.24), and the imagery connected with it stresses debilitation, loss, disorientation, falling. This 'otherness' of Alain's is particularly underlined by Mieke Bal when she isolates the detail of his going back to bed just when other people are getting up, and of his twice appearing in the garden in full daylight in his pyjamas (*15*, pp.27, 75). Such details do more than establish a link with an earlier and more irresponsible state, they set up an alternative order, a set of forces that Alain appears to be responding to in a trance-like compulsion.

So we see an Alain who veers away from serious interaction with others. His mother may be an important element in his life, but we learn that he has very seldom entered her bedroom (2, p.158), and their conversations are few. He is merely comforted by the sound of a voice that he does not interpret, 'voix dont il n'écoutait pas les paroles, murmure affectueux, insignifiant et nécessaire' (p.29). Quoted dialogue with Camille is fairly trite, but he evades the closeness and tensions of anger both lucidly and instinctively. He deliberately manipulates such a scene, either defusing emotion with irony or experiencing boredom and lassitude (p.104), or, as with the evening after Saha's fall, provoking and controlling such an exchange so that a rupture becomes possible; that it was desired is signalled by his surprise at his own failure to cry: '"Je voulais... Ah! oui, je voulais pleurer..." Il sourit et retomba endormi' (p.141).

So why is Alain's relationship with Saha so close? She represents the only free choice he has ever made in his life. He belongs to a social group which has no interest in animals, and his immediate circle is amazed when he returns from the cat-show with the three-month-old captive that he has liberated. Alain too is surprised to find in himself an instinctive understanding of this animal: 'L'admiration et la compréhension du chat, il les portait innées en lui, rudiments qui lui donnèrent, par la suite, de traduire Saha avec facilité' (p.36). In this area alone, his intelligence works energetically, and he even runs to keep pace with her. He is boringly didactic when passing on his heaven-sent knowledge: 'Il lui enseignait les us et les coutumes du félin, comme une langue étrangère riche de trop de subtilités. Malgré lui il mettait, à l'enseigner, de l'emphase' (p.67).

Alone with Saha, however, it is another Alain who emerges, sensitive, alert, imaginative, loving, articulate. Only for her is the discourse of tenderness released, with its familiar rituals: 'Mon petit ours à grosses joues... Fine-fine-fine chatte... Mon pigeon bleu... Démon couleur de perle' (p.21). This is the pattern of his celebratory address to Saha, a series of animal comparisons in his metaphors, and the sense of something alien to which he responds in the 'démon' image, repeated when the cat bites him (p.31), echoed when he gently scolds her in a series of insults, 'ô ma laide, ô ma coureuse sous la pluie, ô ma dévergondée' (p.38). This easy reference to her sexuality contrasts with the stiffening of panic that even the simulated evocation of pregnancy for Camille aroused in him (p.98). But of course it was possible to remove Saha's kittens, restore her to apparent purity, channel her sensuality once more to his own person. This is the kind of control that Léa exerts over Chéri, exulting in his 'otherness', but implicitly denying his independence.

All of Alain's intelligence surfaces and focuses on the investigation of the mystery of Saha's fall. He scrutinises every symptom of her condition with an alert acuity. The suspense that the reader feels is Camille's. She is the 'pauvre petite meurtrière' (p.119) who diminishes as Alain's authority grows. His final terse 'C'est toi, n'est-ce pas? Tu l'as jetée?' (p.132) is not a question, but an assertion, not just a detective triumph but the end of a silent struggle.

Alain is not a complex character, and certainly not self-analytical. But these different perspectives, and his intense inner life, make his a mysterious and disconcerting presence. From the start, critical reception was cool. It is mainly his love for an animal that repelled: 'il faut bien que je dise que j'y vois un peu d'odieux, et souvent, surtout, pas mal de ridicule' said a contemporary critic (*20*), and he added 'Mme Colette est peut-être le type même de l'antihumanisme'. Later critics have been less disturbed by this relationship, but have concentrated more directly on Alain's apparent rejection of normality, his regressive passivity; 'a monstrous denial of the present and the future', Cottrell calls it (*23*, p.106), and Davies underlines the dark undertones of the conclusion: 'Colette leaves us at the end in no doubt that this is an aberration and that Alain is irretrievably lost in his exclusive and impossible love. Like Chéri, he is laid waste by a unique passion' (*24*, p.89).

Alain's personality seems enriched by his reverie and by the intensity of his dream-world. But when one of his dreams is charted, though he may imagine himself to be at ease among a 'foule bénigne' (p.23), it is finally his vulnerability that dominates, as he tries to rationalise the embarrassment of his public nakedness (p.24). For Quilliot, this fey quality, his passivity, and the persistence of sharply-defined childhood images are more easily understood by reference to Colette's second brother Léo, who lived out a solitary life with no human involvement, settled for a monotonous and unrewarding type of employment, failed to develop his musical and imaginative talents, and retained an uncompromising loyalty to the sights and sounds of his childhood. Colette's respect for the integrity of 'le Sylphe' makes it difficult for Quilliot to see Alain as morally or psychologically arrested. Rather, she sees him as an extension of and

comment on certain of Colette's family characteristics: 'les enfants
de Sido se créent tranquillement leurs propres valeurs au mépris du
vulgaire, et ne donnent pas le sens ordinaire aux mots de "réussite"
ou d'"échec"' (*39*).

The text raises problems for more overtly feminist critics; a
first reaction is sympathy for Camille, since she is, after all, treated
brusquely and insensitively. But another urge is identification with
Alain, and this is very likely because of the element of role reversal
and ambivalence in the marriage. A number of Alain's reactions, his
physical reserve, his feeling of being dominated, his fastidiousness,
his link with Nature, these have often been traditionally attributed to
the woman in a relationship, and so the signals of the conclusion
may seem difficult for the reader to accept. Forde and Spencer turn
to the figure of Alain's mother for shreds of hope for Alain's future.
Against Camille's solitary stance, the figure of Alain is bastioned and
extended through his mother and the servants, Saha and the living
entity of the garden. Whereas she is often seen as a mere back-cloth
element, Alain's mother is identified by Spencer as 'one of Colette's
wise women' (*43*). This sets her apart from the usual maternal
presence in Colette's fiction, either non-existent or at best superficial
and inadequate. Certainly Mme Amparat is within the Sido orbit,
loving but discreet, and a devoted gardener. When Alain returns
home with Saha, she does not have the strength to refuse him refuge,
and indeed, in a significant piece of oblique dialogue, appears to
connive at his escape:

> — S'il n'y a pas de draps à mon ancien lit, maman, je
> m'envelopperai dans n'importe quoi...
> — Il y a des draps à ton lit, dit Mme Amparat. (p.139)

But it is through her consciousness that this reintegration of Alain
into the home context can be seen as not necessarily final: 'it is she
who implants in the reader's mind a feeling that Alain's retreat from
life is to be a temporary one' (*43*). If this is not a self-deluding
perception, it does shade off the apparent finality of the conclusion,

and, for Spencer at least, creates more of a link with *La Naissance du jour* than might otherwise be anticipated.

Saha

Colette's last, most celebrated, and most photographed cat, 'la Chatte' or 'la Dernière Chatte', who died in 1939, is acknowledged to be in part a model for Saha. But when Colette celebrates this companion it is for her extraordinary powers of alert, intelligent adaptation to the closed city or hotel life that she led with her growingly crippled mistress. It is her humanisation that Colette never ceases to wonder at, when writing for instance to her friend Hélène Jourdan-Morhange, 'Mais la Chatte est extraordinaire. Elle ne cesse de nous *remercier* de l'avoir emmenée, de nous démontrer qu'elle comprend tout', she writes on a visit to Brussels in 1932 (*14*, p.52), and again in 1936, 'La Chatte bat tous ses records de sociabilité' (*14*, p.110).

But Saha has another kind of identity, and another role to play. Sociable she is not. Her reserved nature and exclusive affections are constantly illustrated: 'Elle n'a aucune notion de l'hospitalité. Regarde comme elle se réjouit du départ de nos amis!' (p.18) comments Mme Amparat. She is exclusive, too, in her identification with the garden, where she mysteriously appears and disappears, a kind of emanation, a spirit of place. We only see her in summer, so her winter habits are unknown, but her presence inside the house is mainly with Alain in his bedroom. The scents of the garden cling to her fur, she snaps up insects, covets birds. The narrative does not analyse her mind or represent her feelings directly; but her movements and experessions, the nuances of her colouring and her voice are described in attentive detail, so that the sense of a subtle and important identity is created. Everybody, even Camille, pays attention to her reactions. Her presence, the shifts of her moods, her swift unpredictable movements are conveyed with a profusion of metaphors, a richness of imagery that no human character in the narrative attracts. Some images ally Saha to the human world, but most underline her links with all the non-human species, mammals, birds, fish, reptiles. She is not a wild creature, but she is firmly inserted into the world of Nature. In her animal sketches and stories Colette often uses humour and irony, particularly when featuring her own pets. This seems to be an instrument both of apprehension and of control. But the tone here is more consistently serious and reflective, and never familiar. No liberties are taken with Saha by this narrator.

Saha is a pedigree Chartreux, her rich fur is 'mauve et bleuâtre comme la gorge des ramiers' (p.33), and her eyes are golden. Secure and at ease while Alain is with her in her garden, she begins to pine as soon as he leaves, and her behaviour towards him changes. Although she always responds, she is more wary and distant when he visits her, and when his concern leads him to take her away to the flat their relationship changes. There is no more playing together, Saha sleeps alone on the bathroom stool that she has selected, she no longer even sits on his lap. But this physical withdrawal does not disarm Camille's mounting frustration. Her resentment is not articulated overtly, it is exteriorised in gestures and glances and tones of voice. Neither is Saha's aloofness defined directly as jealousy or suffering. This narrative even-handedness and restraint gives a kind of parity to these two females. They revolve around Alain, they are 'ses deux captives du belvédère' (p.70). So is prepared the key scene of the physical duel between them, the only scene where Alain is absent. Here the narrative is at its plainest and most economical; Colette follows through all the limited and monotonous movements of the couple with an intent fidelity, from their disarmingly casual beginnings to the unexpected and apparently random moment of Saha's fall. There is no dramatic heightening of Camille's unplanned, almost mechanical actions as she drives the cat to and fro across the narrow balcony, from closed door to parapet and back again, nor is her motivation or intention probed. A more developed understanding of what is at stake is accorded to Saha. Hers is the only cry to break the silence, 'un miaulement long, désolé' (p.112), a recognition that seems to focus Camille's unconsciousness into a more specific resolve. The moment when Saha begins to fear for her life is brilliantly conveyed by the damp prints that she leaves on the hot concrete as her paws start to sweat. Camille is the focaliser of her fall; it has no sequel in the text and we only learn later that it was broken by a second-floor awning:

> Elle eut le temps d'entendre le crissement des griffes sur le torchis, de voir le corps bleu de Saha tordu en S, agrippé à l'air avec une force ascendante de truite, puis elle recula et s'accota au mur. (p.114)

The Saha whom Alain brings back into the flat in his arms is passive, dazed, and in shock. Only her snarl at Camille and the renewed dampness of her pads bear testimony, as does Camille's 'petite voix'. Camille's hysterical tears are misread by Alain as a mark of compassion, and the truth only emerges slowly. Saha cannot make her accusation directly, but 'tout le félin visage s'efforçait avec un langage universel, vers un mot oublié des hommes' (p.121). In this rare moment of lyrical speculation Colette seems to refer most directly to the nostalgia for a lost and mythical unity that pervades this text, and of which Saha is the symbol, 'ta chimère' (p.149), as Mme Amparat calls her. The same poignancy is present in *Le Blé en herbe* (emphasised particularly in the article by Fischler), where the 'fall' itself is enacted.

Restored to her garden, Saha is comforted more rapidly than Alain himself. The next morning she is 'rayonnante ... elle fixait sur le jardin des yeux de despote heureux' (p.143). The final celebrated image of the novel shows a grave Saha observing Camille's departing figure 'humainement', while a crouching Alain plays with the first green chestnuts 'd'une paume adroite et creusée en patte' (p.159).

This is not the only story of Colette's in which a man opts in the end for his animal companion. In 'La Chienne' (*4, Douze dialogues de bêtes*), a soldier on leave divines his mistress's infidelity from the transparent behaviour of the dog that he has confided to her care, and straightaway departs with this candid and loving beast. His need for security is paramount, and only the dog can offer this. This text was first published in 1916, and another, of 1911, 'La Chienne jalouse' (*4, La Paix chez les bêtes*), is an even closer variant to the theme of *La Chatte*, since the narrative vocalises the desperate but controlled jealousy of the bitch towards the woman who has entered her master's life and home: 'Non, tu ne saurais jamais à quelle heure j'ai voulu m'élancer, refermer mes dents sur ta gorge et ne plus bouger et entendre ton sang murmurer comme un ruisseau' (*4*, p.80). The monologue conveys the tensions between her sheepdog instinct of guarding the woman on their walks and the hurt love and hopeless jealousy that burn inside her. But it is of course a humanised discourse. The challenge that Colette took on in *La Chatte* was perhaps a greater one, to make Saha an important character while retaining all her animal features. There are of course moments of anthropomorphic hypothesis in the text, but for the most part emotion is only inferred by the narrator through movements and expressions. But another challenge is to make her at once a believable animal and the vehicle of the text's multiple meanings. She is the source of a delicate eroticism as she kneads Alain's chest in the 'claustral space', as Forde puts it (27), of the bedroom. Her first appearance is not so much as an animal but as an emanation of the night: 'Un reflet d'argent s'élança d'un massif, coula comme un poisson contre les jambes d'Alain' (p.12). Her speech is phoneticised, and only Alain can distinguish between her 'Merrouin', 'Merraing' and 'Mouek'. His attentiveness to her is active, because he realises, intermittently, that she represents 'sa chance d'isolement, son égoïsme, sa poésie' (p.105). But he is not unaware of the doomed nature of his choice.

> Déjà elle embaumait la menthe, le géranium et le buis. Il
> la tenait confiante et périssable, promise à dix ans de vie
> peut-être, et il souffrait en pensant à la brièveté d'un si
> grand amour. (p.140)

It is this awareness that gives an edge of fatality and pathos to the novel's conclusion.

The garden

In one of the sketches of *La Maison de Claudine* Colette recalls her reaction on returning to her provincial home after a fortnight in Paris.

> Ces cubes sans jardins, ces logis sans fleurs où nul chat ne miaule derrière la porte de la salle à manger, où l'on n'écrase pas, devant la cheminée, un coin du chien traînant comme un tapis, ces appartements privés d'esprits familiers, où la main, en quête de cordiale caresse, se heurte au bois, au velours inanimés, je les quittai avec des sens affamés, le besoin véhément de toucher, vivantes, des toisons ou des feuilles, des plumes tièdes, l'émouvante humidité des fleurs. (*4*, pp.998-99)

Yet she was to spend many years of her life in just such deprived Parisian dwellings, although seldom until very late in her life, without animal companionship. But she prized especially the splendid gardens that still remained in the Passy and Neuilly districts, deploring the constant insidious inroads of the developers. 'Le grignotage des parcs privés, à Paris, est à peu près achevé' she wrote in 1944, recalling in *Trois... six... neuf* the whole sequence of her varied Parisian residences. One reminiscence is of her flat in the Rue de Villejust, near the Bois which, in 1906, offered a view of fine old trees, spacious courtyards and gardens, and the sight of Lanka; 'la chatte blanche de Robert d'Humières, descendait de son ciel persan, s'asseyait au centre du massif rose [of campion] et reposait sur toutes choses environnantes le regard de ses yeux surnaturellement bleus' (*11*, p.36). This particular memory of a cat devoted to 'le maître qu'elle aimait d'un amour unique' (*11*, p.37) and reigning over a peaceful luxuriant garden seems very close to *La Chatte*, even to the emphasis on pink flowers. There is campion in the novel too, but another flower attracts Alain's attention more significantly, the pink sage, or salvia, that he recognises almost ecstatically on his return: 'Ce petit massif en forme de cœur, Alain ne l'avait connu que rouge,

et toujours bordé d'héliotropes' (p.145). Even if we do not accept
fully Forde's proposition that this is a direct image of Alain's own
heart 'protected and ensnared in this private space' (27), it is possible
to view this particular enclosed shape as a representation *en abyme*
of the garden itself, especially as it is presided over by an aged and
near-sterile cherry tree.

The features of the garden that are used to create its identity
are the seasonally-blooming beds of flowering plants, the flowering
shrubs and climbers, and the tall, well-established trees. As is her
custom, Colette gives to all of these their botanical names, and in an
otherwise spare and uncluttered narrative the exotic richness of this
terminology seems to contribute to a profound self-renewing and
privileged identity for this garden. Colours, textures, scents are
evoked, night as well as day-time effects, and the succession of the
different flowerings creates a visible time-sequence. Beds of
campion and forget-me-not give place to geraniums and poppies;
exuberant shrubs billow everywhere, deutzia and weigilia, clematis,
wistaria, laburnum, and, most impressive, the great trees. The trees
emerge almost as characters, the fine tulip tree, the dazzling poplar:
'Un seul arbre, un peuplier à jeunes feuilles vernissées, recueillait la
clarté lunaire et dégouttait d'autant de lueurs qu'une cascade' (p.12).
Largest of all are the elms, the enormous survivors of a very different scenario that predates the garden itself, 'reliquats d'une quadruple
et princière avenue' (pp.11-12). When he comes across the dying
yew that has been uprooted by the builders to make way for the
extension Alain mourns as if for a human being, and the theme of
death is most evident in the recurring mention of the unnamed dead
tree which is draped in climbers, honeysuckle, vines and clematis.

A number of critics, Bal in particular, have seen this tree,
together with other signs of vegetable decay, as the clearest of
indications that the garden mirrors Alain's paralysis, and for Maurin
it is part of 'une dialectique du mouvement et de l'immobilité' (35)
that shapes the whole book.

In the active tending of the garden Alain plays no role (thus
confirming the 'immobility' theory), although his mother is endlessly
engaged in shaping and controlling this domain. He is several times

referred to as the prince of this seemingly magical kingdom, but his role is to preside, enjoy, and sense the living fibres of this entity. That we are unaware of its exact extent and configuration, since, as Bal points out (*15*, p.67), we see it only fragmentarily and in close-up through Alain's gaze, simply adds to its mystery and uniqueness. Yet there is a perhaps unexpected link with the Quart-de-Brie, since there too Alain can see further survivors of the depleted tribe: 'Trois hauts peupliers âgés, épaves d'un beau jardin détruit, balançaient leurs cimes à la hauteur de la terrasse' (p.70). In this building, too, we witness Alain's concern for the plants that are imprisoned in their pots on the hot concrete, as he takes the trouble to move them back into the shade (p.51), an instinct to succour that does not extend to his fellow-humans, but parallels his preoccupation with Saha's feeding and temperature.

There are, then, many levels of interpretation in *La Chatte*, and much is only suggested or partly spelt-out. The narrator-figure intervenes less often than in *Le Blé en herbe* to comment from a stance of superior experience or wisdom on the actions or attitudes of the characters, or to link these to some assumed norm of gender-perception. Alain's resentment at Camille's increasing air of softness, plumpness and well-being is called 'l'antique grief viril' (p.96), and the identification of men as short-term sensualists one and all (p.107) is adduced as one reason for lack of understanding between the protagonists. But these are minor elements of narration; the overall attitude is cool, restrained and unjudging. However, this does not, as we have seen, prevent commentators from taking sides passionately on their own account. Not only are there straightforward pro-Alain or pro-Camille camps, but a conviction that we are presented here with extremely superficial characters means that Saha is bound to emerge for some as superior: 'Colette réussit à camper au premier plan la dignité, le mystère de l'animal, dans un univers où l'homme est de la plus stricte indigence' (*33*, p.74). This view, and mistrust of Camille in particular, has a long history, being shared by Marks (1961), Ketchum (1968) and Biolley-Godino (1972). Then there is the temptation of the paradoxes. Perhaps we have here three human beings, as many imply; or is it three animals that Colette wants us to see? Or, by a final twist, are we in the presence of two animals and one human being — Saha (*45*, p.145)?

One thing is certain: it is misleading to look on this as a novel of social comment and realism. A small detail illustrates how important it was to Colette to unify this text and to place everything in the orbit of the main characters. After her fall Saha was (in the *brouillons*) to have been brought back to the flat by a stranger from another storey in the building, but Colette finally chose to have her reappear in Alain's arms. There was to be no intruder in this plot. The dialogue has been reproached for its banality, but another approach would stress the significance of its recurring elements to the overall circular structures. Every feature of speech, action and description carries a resonance beyond the immediate, for this is, as Davies says (*24*, p.85), 'a kind of poetic fable'.

Appendix

Le Blé en herbe

Title in *Le Matin*	Date of publication	Chapter number 1923 edition
'La Crevette'	29 July 1922	I
'Vinca'	2 September 1922	II
'En attendant'	16 September 1922	III
'Daphnis'	30 September 1922	IV
'Drames'	7 October 1922	V
'Sérénité'	14 October 1922	VI
'Les Ombres'	21 October 1922	VII
'L'Antre'	18 November 1922	VIII
'Les Chardons'	9 December 1922	IX
'La Soumission'	23 December 1922	X
'Nocturne'	13 January 1923	XI
'Faiblesse'	17 February 1923	XII
'Pardon'	24 February 1923	XIII
'La Quémandeuse'	10 March 1923	XIV
'La Comparaison'	31 March 1923	XV

Select Bibliography

COLETTE'S WORKS

1. *Le Blé en herbe* (Paris: Garnier-Flammarion, 1969). This edition, with a preface by Claude Pichois, is the one referred to in the text. *Le Blé en herbe* is available in several paperback editions, and the Hodder and Stoughton edition has a comprehensive preface by Brian Stimpson.
2. *La Chatte* (Paris: Livre de poche, 1989).
3. *Œuvres*, I (Paris: Gallimard, Bibl. de la Pléiade, 1984).
4. *Œuvres*, II (Paris: Gallimard, Bibl. de la Pléiade, 1986).
4a. *Œuvres*, III (Paris: Gallimard, Bibl. de la Pléiade, 1991). The Pléiade edition is currently being edited by Claude Pichois, and is lavishly annotated. Vol. III contains *La Chatte*, pp.807-91.
5. *Œuvres complètes*, 15 volumes (Paris: Le Fleuron, 1948-50). This is the edition, revised by Colette, that many of the critics use in their references. As it is out of print, I have preferred to use mainly the Pléiade volumes or more accessible paperbacks.
6. *La Femme cachée* (Paris: Gallimard, Coll. Folio, 1974).
7. *La Naissance du jour* (Paris: Garnier-Flammarion, 1969).
8. *Sido and Les Vrilles de la vigne* (Paris: Livre de poche, 1972).
9. *Mes apprentissages* (Paris: Ferenczi, 1936).
10. *Le Journal à rebours* (Paris: Livre de poche, 1974).
11. *Trois... six... neuf* (Paris: Corrêa, 1944).
12. *Lettres à Marguerite Moreno* (Paris: Flammarion, 1959).
13. *Lettres à ses pairs* (Paris: Flammarion, 1973).
14. *Lettres à Moune et au Toutounet* (Paris: Editions des Femmes, 1985).

SECONDARY REFERENCES

15. Bal, Mieke, *Complexité d'un roman populaire (ambiguïté dans "La Chatte")* (Paris: La Pensée Universelle, 1974). Bal has also published three other important articles.
16. Bazin, André, 'Les Incertitudes de la fidélité', *Cahiers du Cinéma*, Vol. 6, 32 (February 1954), 37-42. A consideration of the relation

between *Le Blé en herbe* and Claude Autant-Lara's film of 1953, with Pierre-Michel Beck, Nicole Berger and Edwige Feuillère.

17. Beaumont, Germaine et Parinaud, André, eds, *Colette par elle-même* (Paris: Seuil, 1951). A warm testimony by Beaumont.

18. Biolley-Godino, Marcelle, *L'Homme-objet chez Colette* (Paris: Klincksieck, 1972). Close analysis of Colette's presentation of the male figure.

19. Bloomberg, Edward, 'Colette et la glycine', *Archiv für das Studium des Neueren Sprachen und Literaturen*, 1 (June 1973), 140-43.

20. Bost, Pierre, *'La Chatte'*, *L'Europe Nouvelle*, 804 (8 July 1933).

21. Bourgogne, Beverly, *'La Chatte* par Colette: "un pas de trois"', *Proceedings of the Pacific N.W. conference on foreign languages, Seattle* (April 1970), 24-26. The triad theory.

22. Carter, Angela, *Nothing Sacred* (London: Virago, 1982). An abrasive, witty essay.

23. Cottrell, Robert, *Colette* (New York: Ungar, 1974). A short, compact, judicious study.

24. Davies, Margaret, *Colette* (Edinburgh: Oliver & Boyd, 1961). An excellent, short, cogent study.

25. Dormann, Geneviève, *Amoureuse Colette* (Paris: Albin Michel, 1984). A somewhat dramatic view of Colette's life, with marvellous photographs.

26. Fischler, Alexander, 'Unity in Colette's *Le Blé en herbe*', *Modern Language Quarterly*, Vol. 3, 2 (June 1969), 248-64.

27. Forde, Marianne, 'Spatial structures in *La Chatte*', *The French Review*, Vol. 58, 3 (February 1985), 360-67.

28. Forestier, Louis, *Chemins vers "La Maison de Claudine" et "Sido"* (Paris:Société d'éditions d'enseignement supérieur, 1968). A suggested structure for these works.

29. Giry, Jacqueline, *Colette et l'art du discours* (Paris: La Pensée Universelle, 1980). One of the few studies of Colette's stylistics.

30. Goudeket, Maurice, *Près de Colette* (Paris: Flammarion, 1956). Invaluable detailed evocation of Colette's latter years.

31. Larnac, Jean, *Colette: sa vie, son oeuvre* (Paris: Kra, 1927).

32. Lefèvre, Frédéric, *Une Heure avec...*, 4e série (Paris: Gallimard, 1927). An interesting interview, where Colette's is the dominant voice.

33. Le Hardouin, Maria, *Colette* (Paris: Editions Universitaires, 1956). A solid general study.

34. Marks, Elaine, *Colette* (London: Secker & Warburg, 1961). Important for the sustained attention that it gives to the works.

35. Maurin, Margaret Simpson, 'Du mouvement et de l'immobilité dans *La Chatte* de Colette', *Dalhousie French Studies*, 6 (Spring-Summer, 1984), 72-83.

36. Mitchell, Yvonne, *Colette, a taste for life* (London: Weidenfeld, 1975). A sympathetic study.

37. Offord, Malcolm, 'Colours in Colette's *Le Blé en herbe*', *Nottingham French Studies*, Vol. 22, 2 (October, 1983).

38. ——, 'Imagery in Colette's *Le Blé en herbe*', *Nottingham French Studies*, Vol. 25, 1 (May 1986) 34-62.

39. Quilliot, Claire, 'Colette, *La Chatte* et le métier d'écrivain', *Revue des Sciences Humaines*, 129 (January-March 1968), 59-77.

40. Resch, Yannick, *Corps féminin, corps textuel* (Paris: Klincksieck, 1973). A close analysis of Colette's images of women.

41. Richard, Jean-Pierre, 'L'Ail et la grenouille', *Nouvelle Revue Française*, 308 (1 September 1978), 99-110. A study of Colette in her childhood and Provençal locales.

42. Sarde, Michèle, *Colette libre et entravée* (Paris: Stock, 1978). The most detailed biography, with a sociological dimension.

43. Spencer, Sharon, 'The Lady of the Beasts: Eros and transformation in Colette', *Women's Studies*, Vol. 8, 3 (1981), 299-312.

44. Stewart, Joan Hinde, *Colette* (Boston: Twayne's Modern Authors, 1983). An excellent concentrated general study.

45. Truc, Gonzague, *Madame Colette* Paris: Corrêa, 1941).

46. Ward Jouve, Nicole, *Colette* (Brighton: Harvester Press, 1987). A compelling meditation on Colette's work and identity.

Since this book went to press two important studies have appeared:

Duffy, Jean, *Colette, 'Le Blé en herbe'* (Glasgow: University of Glasgow French and German Publications, 1989).

Holmes, Diana, *Colette* (Basingstoke and London: Macmillan, 1991).

CRITICAL GUIDES TO FRENCH TEXTS

edited by
Roger Little, Wolfgang van Emden, David Williams

1. **David Bellos.** Balzac: La Cousine Bette.
2. **Rosemarie Jones.** Camus: L'Etranger *and* La Chute.
3. **W.D Redfern.** Queneau: Zazie dans le métro.
4. **R.C. Knight.** Corneille: Horace.
5. **Christopher Todd.** Voltaire: Dictionnaire philosophique.
6. **J.P. Little.** Beckett: En attendant Godot *and* Fin de partie.
7. **Donald Adamson.** Balzac: Illusions perdues.
8. **David Coward.** Duras: Moderato cantabile.
9. **Michael Tilby.** Gide: Les Faux-Monnayeurs.
10. **Vivienne Mylne.** Diderot: La Religieuse.
11. **Elizabeth Fallaize.** Malraux: La Voie Royale.
12. **H.T Barnwell.** Molière: Le Malade imaginaire.
13. **Graham E. Rodmell.** Marivaux: Le Jeu de l'amour et du hasard *and* Les Fausses Confidences.
14. **Keith Wren.** Hugo: Hernani *and* Ruy Blas.
15. **Peter S. Noble.** Beroul's Tristan *and the* Folie de Berne.
16. **Paula Clifford.** Marie de France: Lais.
17. **David Coward.** Marivaux: La Vie de Marianne *and* Le Paysan parvenu.
18. **J.H. Broome.** Molière: L'Ecole des femmes *and* Le Misanthrope.
19. **B.G. Garnham.** Robbe-Grillet: Les Gommes *and* Le Voyeur.
20. **J.P. Short.** Racine: Phèdre.
21. **Robert Niklaus.** Beaumarchais: Le Mariage de Figaro.
22. **Anthony Cheal Pugh.** Simon: Histoire.
23. **Lucie Polak.** Chrétien de Troyes: Cligés.
24. **John Cruickshank.** Pascal: Pensées.
25. **Ceri Crossley.** Musset: Lorenzaccio.
26. **J.W Scott.** Madame de Lafayette: La Princesse de Clèves.
27. **John Holyoake.** Montaigne: Essais.
28. **Peter Jimack.** Rousseau: Emile.
29. **Roger Little.** Rimbaud: Illuminations.